THE **CEO'S PLAYBOOK**

THE
CEO'S
PLAYBOOK

*Turning the Employees You Have
into the Dream Team
You Always Wanted*

BY NORA GANESCU, PhD

NEW YORK

NASHVILLE • MELBOURNE • VANCOUVER

THE **CEO'S PLAYBOOK**

Turning the Employees You Have into the Dream Team You Always Wanted

Published in New York, New York, by Morgan James Publishing in partnership with Difference Press

The Morgan James Speakers Group can bring authors to your live event. For more information or to book an event visit The Morgan James Speakers Group at www.TheMorganJamesSpeakersGroup.com.

ISBN 978-1-68350-310-1 paperback
ISBN 978-1-68350-312-5 eBook
ISBN 978-1-68350-311-8 hardcover
Library of Congress Control Number: 2016917111

Cover Design by:
Chris Treccani
www.3dogdesign.net

Interior Design by:
Chris Treccani
www.3dogdesign.net

In an effort to support local communities, raise awareness and funds, Morgan James Publishing donates a percentage of all book sales for the life of each book to Habitat for Humanity Peninsula and Greater Williamsburg.

Get involved today! Visit
www.MorganJamesBuilds.com

Dedication

To Guido and David, with all my love.

Table of Contents

Introduction

Work is love made visible. And if you can't work with love,
but only with distaste, it is better that you should leave
your work and sit at the gate of the temple and take alms
of the people who work with joy.
–Kahlil Gibran

* * *

know we haven't met, but here is a bet I am willing to make:
You are highly intelligent person, and you deeply care about
your company and its mission. How do I know that? I work
with CEOs all the time (so I have my personal research sample),
and I also know that you have proven your ability many times
along the way to get this job. Or maybe you even built up the
company yourself, and the proof is in the fact that you're still
growing and competing.

In my career, I have worked with many people like you,
and it's pretty awesome. I am always eager to work with smart,
talented people with a vision and the means and tenacity to
make it happen. The CEOs are dedicated doers, no question

about it. Yet, these awesome people have a collective but also secret burning question: "If I am so smart, why can't I get the people in my company to give their very best – consistently?"

Of course, you are right. What your senses and intuition tell you is recently confirmed by research: 70% of the entire workforce either doesn't care much about their work (just put in the hours, go through the moves), or actively resists, even boycotts what you are trying to accomplish. Disengagement of some 70% is very bad news, and this is not the number estimated for the worst companies, it's an *average* company in 2016. Maybe the only solace I can offer you is that you are not alone. This burning question (as in, an urgent burning in both your soul and your bottom line) has also been my core question my entire career. This is what I set out to answer:

How can we be at our best together? How can we maximize our individual and collective performance, and approach our work with joy and ease?

I am happy to report that after 25 years of inquiry, work, and trial and error, I think I have figured it out. This is what this book is about: permanently removing that issue that has confounded you for so long from your problems list.

It turns out that the solution to our growing disengagement is both incredibly challenging and mind-blowingly easy.

Challenging, because you'll have to drop some beliefs that are in your way – by this I mean the stuff, thoughts, assumptions, and conclusions that we learn to take for granted, even if they are not true or useful.

Easy, because once you understand how engagement works, it takes significantly less effort (though most of us resist because we believe it will require so much more).

This book offers a blueprint for this transformation journey.

Chapter 1 looks into what is actually happening in companies. Not only that which has created such a widespread, global work "malaise" in recent years, but also the work environment of today and tomorrow. There have been tremendous changes that have affected the world of work, and it looks like there is no turning back. We need to reset our assumptions about today's work landscape and culture.

Chapter 2 looks into what is possible. Where should we go from here, in the way we think about and organize work in our companies? What is our vision for how we want to relate to our people, and how we want them to relate to us?

Chapters 3 to 5 lead you through a vision of the journey from where you are now to where you want to be: in a company of people who care deeply about their work and show up at their best every single day. You will learn the very specific steps and concrete actions that you need to take, and who to involve to help with this effort.

Chapter 6 offers you several useful tools that will make the journey easy, enjoyable, and effective.

Last, but not least, Chapter 7 offers more ideas about where can you go to help establish a new culture of work in your company, and what additional support is available to you if you want to go deep to apply these principles in your teams.

This book stands on the shoulders of many wonderful and pioneering thinkers, practitioners, colleagues, and peers, all of whom have fought to figure out how very different people can work together for their own benefit – and the benefit of their community. Their ideas, examples, and tools have inspired me, taught me, and enriched my experience. In particular, I am grateful for my mentors and peers from the Art of Hosting community, and the learning community that started around Frederic Laloux's amazing book, *Reinventing Organizations*.

Now, it is my turn to share what I have learned from my mentors, colleagues, and, above all, my clients. I hope that you will enjoy reading this book, and especially applying it, because you and your people are awesome – and your precious gifts and time would be terrible to waste.

We figured out the alchemy, now let us create gold together. There's plenty for everyone.

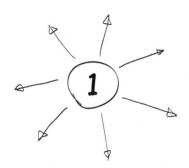

FIXING THE
"PEOPLE ISSUES"

The man in front of me looked exasperated. His attempt to unify and excite his employees wasn't working, and it was bleeding vital energy out of him and his company.

"All I want is that people *care*," he said. "That they show up to work and feel good about it, because it is a good thing that we are trying to do here. We're offering great products and services. We're growing, at least we were. . . . Instead, what do I get? This never-ending stream of 'people issues' keeps me up at night. There is so much we could achieve together, and yet, many days I cannot shake the feeling that these people would rather be anywhere else. You can feel it in the air, the moment you step in the office."

Dan, a 41-year-old CEO, called me for help, and this was the scene at our initial strategy session. He was frustrated, and it wasn't for lack of trying. Dan had tried everything he could think of: teambuilding sessions, super-detailed job descriptions, lengthy guidelines, new procedures, better feedback, visible posters with the company vision in all the rooms – he had even recommended and paid for motivational workshops for some of his people. He had let the people who were not performing go (even if it was difficult for everybody involved), had hired very, very selectively to replace them, and had carefully bought and installed an enterprise social platform that was said to help with communication and knowledge-sharing. Then, he had conducted an "engagement survey."

He felt alone in caring really deeply about the company, its mission, and its future, as well as what it felt like to spend five (sometimes six) days a week under that roof. Meanwhile, the people around him seemed either "just not that into" the work or the team, or somehow afraid.

Dan was used to having to figure things out. This company was at the center of his life, and he wished nothing more than that the 132 people working with him would feel fully or even partially committed to their work during the time they were at the office. Yet, that dream felt out of reach. Maybe with this business, he thought, with these people, in this location, this was just not possible. How very frustrating, considering the waste of energy, of money, and of possibilities. Frustration and a sense of anxiety about the future were getting to him daily. Because, he sensed, if it's not getting better, it will probably get worse.

Dan is not a pessimistic person, nor someone who would give up easily or be reticent to take on challenges. He created his company in his 20s, and then grew it over the past 15 years to its current 132 employees. He was something of a thought leader in his industry, and by all signs he was a very accomplished businessman by this time. Getting to know him, I learned he was indeed a highly intelligent, warm, and caring person, a good friend, and a doting father. He truly cared about the people around him, about the environment, and about the future of the planet. He believed in learning and improving all the time, but somehow, this problem stumped him like no other.

Dan's "people problem" was way more confusing than other business decisions, and he felt he was missing a clear, tested, and proven course of action. Surely, there would be one. Even the questions swirling around in his head were contradicting each other. On the one hand, was it a big deal if people didn't really *like* the work? Isn't that *normal*? Don't people work because they *have to,* not because they *like to*? Wasn't that just too much to realistically expect – well, as long as they still showed up and showed a decent effort? Maybe being excited every day (or even most days) about what you do for a living is a luxury reserved to the lucky few (and he was one of those).

It was fairly easy to explain away his own expectations and observations as being beyond his control. Then again, what happened to all that excitement and enthusiasm people showed when he hired them? He was always very careful to hire good people who genuinely wanted to be part of the bigger work of the company. Was the missing piece of his management style – the one that made it impossible for him to crack this piece of the puzzle – putting the entire company in danger? Was it his fault? Was there a possibility to feel better and do significantly better by increasing his employees' dedication and commitment to the company, or was that just a pipe dream?

I tell you about Dan because, while he is an actual person (his name has been changed), he is also such a typical portrait of the people who consult with me. I can easily imagine that, even if you haven't yet tried every trick in the book, you'll be able to relate to his experience as a leader.

So I will tell you just what I told him. Two key things up front. First: You are *not* alone. Second: You *can* get your people to love to come to work and do their very best, joyfully, every day. I dedicate much of this book to the theory and concrete steps that enable you to do exactly that. For now, I would like to spend a little time on the first point, for it sheds light on why these problems show up in your business at all.

You are not alone. Actually this is a huge understatement. According to the most comprehensive study on this topic conducted by Gallup, about 70% of all employees in the US, Europe, and around the world would rather not be at their job. They are physically showing up there, going through the moves, doing what they need to not get fired. *But that is all.* The bare minimum. A significant number of them, about 20% of the total number of employees (one in five!) on a typical work team, is actually actively sabotaging their workplace with gossip, intrigues, deliberate delays, shoddy work, etc. The opposite of creating value – they are actively damaging the business they work for. As you can see, a company where people are excited about their job is actually a rare (but very beautiful) thing. Only 30% of all employees are fully engaged at work (but they *do* exist).

At one time, everyone dreamed of getting along and being productive at work. Many CEOs have given up on that dream. They resign themselves to the soul-sucking drudgery of endless, seemingly uphill effort, pushing conflict resolutions, disaster responses, and mediocre (at best) results in the end. But the costs of that resignation are staggering. They are debilitating for the CEOs, for the businesses they run, and far beyond that.

What are those costs? When companies and organizations fail to bring out the best in their people, they lose enormous amounts of money. The famous Gallup Research Institute estimates that active disengagement (i.e., those people who are counterproductive to the company's objectives) costs the US economy $450 billion to $550 billion per year. For your company, it could be as high as a third of your payroll cost, a figure that is the true for the average, "typical" company. They fail to attract and keep the best people in the business. Even more significantly, they miss out on innovation and creativity, fresh ideas that would make the business sustainable and competitive.

The highest cost, however, is the one everybody in the company pays every day of their lives: not enjoying it. Disliking something we spend hours doing every day has huge medical and mental care costs that put a strain on families and communities. Not coming fully alive at your workplace, literally wilting away your talents, stops being an isolated, individual problem. It is a societal syndrome with global, harrowing effects on people, families, and the economy.

But where does this come from? Was it always like this? What has changed? What is wrong with "those people"?

Yes! It has changed. Almost everything has changed.

New Times, New People

First, there is a significant generational change. The way young people (and here I'll include most people under 45) experience the world has profoundly changed. There are many studies about what this means. Here are the most important points in a nutshell:

Autonomy, independence and collaboration: While people of all ages like to be valued and want their ideas to be used, Generations Y and Z (Millennials and Digital Natives) take this for granted. They are not interested in a traditional career ladder, and will frequently change jobs if their experience contradicts this expectation. Less than life-work balance, they want a fulfilling *life,* and work is cast as just a part of it. Most importantly, they believe that this is possible for them.

They are connected like never before. They rely on information from inside and outside of the company. They have a hard time with hierarchical titles and positions, and they will go straight to the decision-makers when they see a problem.

They want autonomy and collaboration. They are amazingly innovative and collaborative, and the youngest among them, especially, have amazing skills to deal with curating and making sense of great amounts of data.

The unprecedented access to technology and the social media connectedness of this generation have shaped these attitudes and behaviors.

They care about the world. Since you may be from one of these generations or close to it, you probably understand exactly what I'm talking about. Globalization has brought us much closer together, and increased our awareness of how we all are interconnected. Whether through the way our products are sourced, the common entertainment we can enjoy, or the environmental disasters that affect all of us, it is clear that the world is more accessible than it felt to previous generations when they were growing up. These new generations question the practices of a company much more readily. They are less intimidated by authority, and less afraid to call it out. It's easy to dismiss them as idealist youth, but there is evidence that this isn't just a fad they will grow out of.

The young people of today have different goals than their parents. Being themselves, **exploring their passions is very important.**

They will not happily play a very narrow role in a company that has perfected the culture of the "human resource" and treats people like disposable spare parts in a machine (a.k.a. still the majority of the corporations operating today). They will, early on, spot the office politics and shadow power structures. If they cannot easily game the system, they will check out internally and stop caring – very soon.

Young people, much more self-confident and outspoken than any other generation before, are rebelling against this. What they want is not some hippie dream of achieving total consensus. They have seen that fail, too. They are looking to work and contribute their best in a company that will not suffocate their individual drive and creativity, and they are looking to be rewarded for their contributions, not for waiting their turn.

You can think of these trends as trouble. Many companies do. But that would be an unfortunate choice. These new generations are increasingly the most qualified and numerous people available, and they are also tremendously resourceful, creative, and innovative. Indeed, they are the *only* people capable of bringing your business into the future in all respects. It's a much better choice to see them as bringing amazing opportunity and potential.

And now: Plenty *hasn't* changed. Not significantly, anyway, over the last century. The dominant thinking about managing people in companies has not changed. In broad lines, this management model will look at a company as some kind of machine or apparatus that has to be made efficient with the same strategies. This machine is built from pieces that are interchangeable and molded to be very similar so they fit in – and don't break the machine. These parts are the so-called human resources, the people.

However, as Dan (and if you are reading this book, probably you too) eventually noticed, running this machine has become more and more difficult, exhausting, and expensive. Many CEOs I meet are confused and highly uncomfortable about this. They would like the problem to go away. In moments of reflection, they know that this culture change is not going anywhere.

Yet as they consider doing something and updating parts of the way they think about employees and workplace culture so that they have a model that works in the new millennia, they are abandoning it all mid-thought. I wouldn't be surprised if you, like they, might feel discouraged before you can even start.

There are some very persistent myths out there that will discourage you and set you up for failure, if you believe them. Here are some of the most common.

A Short Mythology

You can't make everybody happy all the time. While this is technically true, it also completely misses the point. You want people to excel, to give their best on a consistent basis. They will do that, even on the days where they are not so happy. Just as a committed parent will give their best to their child even on the days when they are not so happy. It's not about happiness but about a company, a team that appreciates and welcomes them with all they have to offer, not just one narrow skill.

Creating the kind of company where people thrive is expensive and risky. Only very rich companies can afford it. Actually, it is much more risky *not* to create one. The opportunity cost businesses pay in lost productivity and innovation is among the highest risk there is for a sustainable future. It doesn't have to be expensive. Most of the changes will cost you nothing. *Not making them* will cost you great amounts of money every day.

Go to the additional resources page on www.theceosplaybook.com to find a calculator that will help you calculate exactly how much time and money this problem wastes in your company every year.

Dealing with "how the employees feel" is a job for the HR department. In actual fact, that is the best way to not achieve anything but spend money nevertheless. Unless you only want to pay lip-service and convey that you are not serious about tackling this problem, don't give it to the HR department to implement. For reasons I will go into later, you are the only one who can solve this.

There is no hard data to demonstrate that companies with excited and engaged people are doing better. Wrong. There is plenty of research and data to back it up.

Changing the way your employees relate to your company is among the changes with highest return on investment, if you do it right. Here is an interesting statistic from the Gallup Research Institute: When companies successfully engage their employees, they experience a 240% boost in performance-related business outcomes, as compared with companies that don't.

I want to pause here and say that if you, like Dan, feel confused and discouraged about that entire topic, I don't blame you. Between the changes that are happening (fast), the outdated thinking about these topics – sometimes from the very sources we would expect to show us the way, such as business schools and consultants, and the persistent myths about how to correct the problem of alienation and disengagement, it is very easy to feel overwhelmed.

This is what most CEOs feel. They turn their attention to something less confusing, maybe a spreadsheet. They try harder at whatever they were doing, and get discouraged when their idea (or gimmick from the latest conference) doesn't work. They rationalize that this what people are, they have always been like this, and they'll always be like that, period. They watch in profound exhaustion and sometimes despair when some of the best people quit. They stagnate and blame it on the industry, the economy, employees, and everybody else. They hope some of their people will "grow up" one day.

I want you to be one of those people who has the courage to choose the more rewarding and – ultimately, the much, much easier – way. You need courage, because doing something new, even thinking some new thoughts, requires courage. I want you to *choose*. I want you to dare to create a simpler and more productive work environment for your employees, and to dare to question some of the "wisdom" you take for granted, ideas that are no longer serving you and your company.

There is no turning back on this endeavor. These problems will not be going away, and ignoring them puts your life's work, your business, in danger. I invite you, instead, to join the tribe of those who changed the way they thought about management and people – and as a result, they changed the way their employees related to them, felt about work, and achieved results for their company. Yes, the old times are gone. The new times, if you prepare for them, can be much better for you and everybody involved.

What will it look like when you get there? That is for you to find out, but the next chapter should give you a glimpse of that destination.

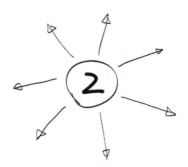

TO LOSE THE FEAR

Everything that is great and inspiring is created by the individual who can labor in freedom.

–Albert Einstein

* * *

What does success look like for you? What would bring a sparkle to your eyes and fill your heart? When it comes to your company, I will venture to say that success involves making it thrive, more relevant, and more sought-after on the market. Success also means delivering on the vision of the company, creating the change in the world that you set out to achieve. All this while enjoying the other things in your life that matter to you. All this while you get to invest your energy in the work that you are most passionate about.

My CEO clients are all committed to their companies. They are happy to show up every day and give their best. So much so that they would be quite anxious at the prospect of not having to show up every single day. They think of their company as a beautiful vehicle in which they create value for the world, for customers, for employees and for themselves. So naturally, they are worried when this beautiful and efficient vehicle is broken. Instead of giving them a great ride, a beautiful experience, and taking them places they desire to go, it seems like a wreck.

But here is the thing: While you are at working "fixing your car," metaphorically, so that you get back to cruising on the highway, you may have completely missed that you are not *on* the highway anymore. Not only is the road unkempt, it is actually ceasing to resemble a serviced road at all. Now you are in the middle of the forest, with no road ahead and no good vehicle. You realize that your maps are outdated, and while you have a good idea about where you would like to end up, your ideas about how to get there will most likely *not* work.

This is the point where I meet many of my potential clients. The way they describe their wish is the equivalent of, "Can you please fix my car? I want to drive fast, and straight to my goal." Many consultants will promise you just that. "Fixing your car" is also the solution that most "people management" courses aim to teach.

Much of that advice is good and, if implemented, will work for a while. As you might have guessed from my car metaphor, it will not work in the wilderness: the fast-changing, globalized, digitalized environment of today and tomorrow, with Generation Xers, Millennials, and Digital Natives working together.

What if you could reimagine and reconstruct what *used to be* "your car" into something else, a new type of vehicle that could continually sense and make sense of the environment? Imagine there was actually a new type of machine that could heal itself when necessary, and have the intelligence to not only help you figure out how to get to your goal, but could also show you worthwhile, achievable goals that you might have missed out on pursuing. This machine would be something that could adapt easily, and care about you as well as about its own integrity, like a sentient being with many (super) powers.

That can be your company. I offer to you the notion that this could be your new definition of success. You don't need a "new car" or a "fixed" car for a cruise on the highway (because there is no highway to the destination anymore), but instead, a select team of super heroes – and their invented vehicles straight out of Marvel – who will give you the ride of your life.

If you believe that this vision is too good to be true (as in the super heroes in Marvel are not real, you know?) it is most probably because you haven't yet heard about an entire class of companies and organization around the world that work this way already. They are in every industry and on all continents. Some are start-ups, and some have transformed themselves from very old-fashioned enterprises or even bureaucracies. Some have only a couple dozen employees, others have hundreds of thousands.

Their stories are well-documented in great books such as Frederic Laloux's *Reinventing Organizations* or Brian M. Carney and Isaac Getz's *Freedom Inc*. These companies are very real, with real people – not "perfect" ones – in real-world markets, not idealized case studies. Yet, they equipped themselves with greater capacity to address and solve the challenges they encounter. They are more flexible, more intelligent, and above all, fully committed down to the last person.

They're also healthier, more relaxed, more innovative, and more playful. What makes them so special, you ask me? Their secret (not that they try to keep any of this for themselves) is that they turn a couple of fundamental assumptions about how to manage people upside-down. With a new set of core beliefs, they can adopt new ways of managing their employees.

Basic Assumptions Challenged

This fundamental rethinking is, for example, the equivalent of Google designing a self-driving car (and changing the future of the cars and transportation).

While all the traditional car manufacturers build their concept vehicles on the dual premises that the human driver is essential and that all systems in the car are designed to help the driver, the Google car sees the driver as the biggest liability for safety – and strives to *completely eliminate* it, potentially saving hundreds of thousands of lives every year. Whatever you think of this particular example, you surely get my point. If the goal was to transport people from A to B with maximum safety and comfort, then the self-driving car might achieve that goal far better than anything on the market before.

What Google did was to turn one of the fundamental assumptions we had about cars, indeed the whole concept of driving, on its head. They weren't afraid to question the basics, possibly because they weren't a car manufacturer, and as such they were not so invested in the old thinking.

When it comes to management and getting the best out of people, these companies have also challenged some fundamental assumptions in those domains. The first one is about the fundamental nature of the human being. The second is about *why* we work.

The Fundamentals

The first step is to recognize that most of the theories we have about management have been have been developed on 150-year-old views of "the worker" as lazy and unreliable. The entire factory system was therefore developed to control and standardize every move of the employee, making him neither more or less than an unassuming and reliable part of the machine.

Adam Smith, the father of the Industrial Revolution and the idea of division of labor, has famously said: "The man whose whole life is spent in performing a few simple operations, of which the effects are perhaps always the same or very nearly the same, has no occasion to exert his understanding or to exercise his invention in finding out expedience for removing difficulties which never occur. He naturally loses, therefore, the habit of such action and generally becomes as stupid and ignorant as it is possible for a human creature to become."

The dominant management thinking in the last century was built on this premise. The employees have to be managed, given direction, and assigned very specific tasks. They have to be controlled, measured, coerced, and incentivized, otherwise they would not work. But is this premise true? Just think about yourself, and about the people around you that you know well, i.e., your family and friends.

I can bet that you will come to the conclusion that generally, it is not true for you and yours. Well, as it turns out, it is not true for the most of the people in this day and age. Still, these outdated attitudes define how we think about managing people. How you see this basic premise is reflected in all the "boarding school" aspects of the workplace: strict working hours, locked storage rooms, restricted access to meetings but obligations to attend other meetings – and ever more time and money invested to control, measure, and police.

Same story when it comes to the fundamental question: Why do people work? The traditional assumption is that people will only work *for pay*. While making decent money is a basic given condition, people will rarely perform at their best just because of it. Yet because of this premise, we make the *money* the most powerful – and sometimes the only – incentive. It is a dearly held old belief, but it is simply not true or effective. What *is* true is that people have an innate desire to create and contribute, and some conditions are conducive to it, while some others may hinder it.

What Do People Want?

Do you want to know what engages people? It is easy to answer that, because there is actually quite some substantive research on this topic (Daniel Pink's book, *Drive,* is a great resource on this). The top three things that will keep people in your company eager to contribute their best talents are (drum roll....) autonomy, mastery, and purpose. Let me say some words about them.

Autonomy. Which kind of task would be more exciting to you: one that you choose and then get to take most of the decisions about, or one where you have almost nothing to decide, and just have to do it? I am talking here about all kinds of decisions, some strategic ones and some smaller tactical decisions. Which one is more of your "baby," the task that will get your full attention and heart? If you're like most people, it is the first one, the one where you get to decide – and if you don't feel competent, then you get to ask advice and then decide – how it gets done. Staff autonomy can sound scary for managers, whose job is traditionally to take away much of the autonomy of the employees.

We are conditioned to think that it will lead to cost and failure. The opposite is true. Imagine, for a moment, what your company might achieve if all of the decisions were to be taken by the people who care most about the outcomes, and are most competent to make them. They would be taken quickly and efficiently, i.e., without wasting people's energy on endless meetings and briefings. How much better, and more enthusiastically, would such decisions be implemented if they were made by the people themselves?

If there could be a way to do that, and guarantee that there is no chaos or abuse, how much easier and better would the work be?

Mastery. It turns out that people like to be good, and to become even better. Of course, nobody's a master in the beginning. If you are not yet very good at something, you will want to do something that you are drawn to, something you are curious and passionate about. That excitement will ensure that you will spend the time and energy it takes in the workplace (and outside of it) to become expert. Improving every day, building on the skills you have and refining them, is not the chore we are led to assume. It is actually one of the things that motivates us most.

What if your company could be the place where people would feel called and supported to pursue mastery in whatever they do? Just imagine what that would mean for your results and your performance.

Purpose. Coming together in the pursuit of something truly worthwhile is what we all want. We all want to invest our time in something meaningful, something that makes a difference. The research confirms this. No matter how trivial the actual task, if we can link it to a worthwhile purpose, we will feel more excited and dedicated to it.

The often quoted parable of the two stone masons comes to mind. In it, two stone masons working on a construction site are asked what it is they are doing. One explains, "I am cutting a block of stone, of rectangular shape: three feet wide, two feet high, and two feet deep." The other one answers simply, "I am building a cathedral." We now know that the second mason will be the one more dedicated and more committed to his work. What is your cathedral? How are you enriching and changing the world with your company? Empty vision statements that are crafted by consultants and splashed on the website – but don't mean really much to anybody – have given mission statements a bad name. It doesn't have to be like this (indeed, you should make sure that this is not the case). Connecting to your highest purpose is what will liberate your Marvel-like super powers. This is also true for your people.

This is, in a nutshell, what those companies who transformed themselves from a car into a Marvel super hero fleet actually did. They had the courage to re-examine and even outright abandon some old and false assumptions – and proceed according to what they knew better to be true. They created cultures based on trust, because, to quote one of their CEOs, "Control is good, but trust is so much better." So pronounces Jean-Francois Zobrist.

His former company, FAVI, is a French foundry that employs 500 people. This was a very traditionally managed company until the year 1983, when Jean-Francois Zobrist was hired to be the new CEO of the company. After a year observing and listening to people, Zobrist decided to fundamentally change the way Favi's work is organized. The two guiding values of the company are now: "the people are good," and "all for the love of the client." He initiated a system in which people have a high degree of freedom. The people in the factory are now self-organizing in teams (called mini-factories) according to the clients they serve. Since they are serving the automotive industry, you would have, for example, a Mercedes-Benz team, a BMW team, a Ford team. They elect their team leader, who has a coordinating role among these teams. Many traditional management and HR roles are distributed within the team, such as making the work schedules, hiring, etc.

FAVI's people take extraordinary responsibility for each other, for their clients, and for constantly innovating and improving. This is not because these people are special, but because the environment is such that it brings out their best qualities.

Most of the team conflicts, when they arise, are solved within the team. The results have been amazing. FAVI has remained the market leader in an industry where the competition has largely moved to China due to price pressure. They command higher prices, but due to the exceptional quality and service they offer, they've maintained their position over 20 years. The employees are enjoying high levels of both autonomy and wellness, as they choose to show up and work as hard as it takes to create excellent work and service. They are also earning wages above the usual market rates in their industry.

The changes initiated by Jean-Francois Zobrist led to the development of a company where people compete to be hired, and most stay for decades. They created a company that is renowned for business success, as well as a great place to work and a community to be part of. This is one example of many.

These companies are very diverse in every respect: size, industry, ownership, sector, or country. Their specific management practices are also different, as they develop their own ways of doing things (often with the participation of their employees). However, they have in common a couple of patterns that Frederic Laloux calls "evolutionary breakthroughs" in his book, *Reinventing Organizations*:

- [ ] A high degree of self-organization. Some of the companies have completely renounced the traditional hierarchy and management, while some have transformed it. In every situation, however, the employees have great deal of freedom and decision-making power within the scope of their work. If that sounds like chaos to you, don't worry; we'll get into the specifics of how that could look in practical terms in the later chapters.

- [ ] An environment of wholeness: People are invited with all the gifts and passions they bring; they are welcome to be who they are. Sometimes that will mean that they can take up a variety of roles in the organization at the same time. Wholeness also means creating an environment that is healthy and respectful towards the people who work within it.

- [ ] The company has an "evolutionary purpose." Like a living being, it will be able to sense and to decide what is the next right thing to do. This stands in opposition to the traditional companies that behave like machines, in which employees (or managers believe the employees) need to be told what the next step should be.

How do these companies perform on the market? Far above average, to tell the truth. When I talk about it, I admit that I get many skeptical looks. Then, because you can't contradict the facts, and the life and work of FAVI and many other very well-documented cases, I get to hear all of the excuses known to man about why this approach couldn't work elsewhere:

☐ Oh, sure, that works in Europe, or in France, but it would never work in the US (or Austria or Slovakia, China, etc., just substitute any other country). Or…

☐ This would never work with us because our people are not used to this, not expecting this.

☐ Our people are not highly educated (or, they are all very highly educated).

☐ Our people are too old/ too young.

☐ We don't have this tradition in our country.

☐ If it is so great, why is it not taught in the business schools?

This is a small selection of the types of reactions (and excuses) that I hear.

Of course, I could labor on contradicting all this, mentioning that such companies who move away from command and control, and give their employees more autonomy, mastery, and purpose – while still a small minority – have successfully functioned, some for decades, in all the industries and on all continents.

I could mention that their internal functioning is well-documented, providing us with a well of learning and inspiration. I could try to convince them that we actually know how to do this! But mostly, I say none of this, for two reasons: Firstly, it is exhausting trying to convince people who are deeply committed to their truth, the old and traditional management assumptions. Secondly, it turns out that they are also right. These assumptions are social theories, not natural laws. If we deeply believe in them, they will shape our reality and perspective. We will interpret our results based on our assumptions going in to the experiment.

When people are committed to seeing their employees as unreliable or untrustworthy, they'll shape their actions and their company norms accordingly, and their experience will confirm what they already know. The employees will "rise" to the level set for them. If they believe that trusting people is a recipe for disaster, the leaders will end up sabotaging any trust-building or trust-based initiative that anybody will suggest. They are right, it will not work for them, because they do not expect it can.

Instead, I am looking for conversations with those people, those CEOs in particular, that recognize in their hearts and minds that this is a much more elegant and powerful path for them, for their company, and for their people. Those who are curious, inspired, and intrigued. If you are one of those people, this book is for you. The next chapters will give you the outline of the requirements to get started and a framework for how to get there, to own your very own superpower, and achieve the cultural rewards of transforming an old style "car" into the Marvel vehicle fleet of the future.

START AT THE HEART
(OF THE MATTER)

Our levels of success will rarely exceed our levels of personal development because success is something we attract by who we become.

– Seth Godin

* * *

n my conversations with CEOs who are inspired and eager for theirs to become the kind of company where everybody's brain and heart is dedicated to its success, we always arrive to the point when the CEO will ask me the question, "Wow, great. Does this mean that you will come and work with my people?"

By work, they mostly mean facilitate some training or workshop, although deep in their hearts they know that no one- or two-day training of any kind can deliver such a transformation. My answer to that question is, without a doubt, "no," or more exactly, "not right away." We might, at a future point, do some great stuff with your employees – but that would be the cherry on the top. Right now, we have to start with the most important success factors, and the factor *who* is also the biggest risk in the whole transformation – and that is you, the CEO.

If you have your own foundations set right for this work, everything else will be easy and obvious. Everything else will be *techniques*. We will talk about what to do in great detail in later chapters, but you can take my word for it right now that the biggest difference between the success stories, and those that fail after a couple of half-hearted attempts, is the behavior of the CEO.

Now, some of my CEOs receive this as bad news, or even get offended.

All it means is that this is not something you can outsource, not something you can get done by others. Also, working on *ourselves* is possibly the most difficult work there is. I see it, however, as great news. It is great news because, really, the only person you will ever control and fully influence is yourself – so that means that the most important part of this work is fully within your power, and within your reach.

If this is the kind of company you want to have, you can totally do it. Some of my skeptics ask, "Does it then not depend on my employees? How come they are not important?" Well, they are important – and how exactly your company will work together will be of your collaborative design – but I have to stop and declare you can get there with the *exact* team that you are employing right now (and I say this not knowing anything about them) and you could *also* get there with a set of completely different employees. As long as you know what you are doing, and you stand by it, it will work.

This chapter is dedicated to your journey, of becoming the kind of CEO that can initiate and support the new ways of working together in the company with ease and grace. You might, understandably, wonder why is it so important to focus on *you*. You weren't exactly lacking in commitment until now, either. *Yet it is.* The best metaphor for your job is that of a gardener. While the gardener cannot create a garden without plants, his job is essential to create the conditions for the plants to grow and bloom.

Without a gardener, there will still be plants: some will thrive, some will die, but you will not have an intentional garden that will serve the purpose that you want it to serve. Your job, as the gardener of your company, is to create the conditions for your people to show up at their best. When they do, many of the hard business decisions that you need to make now, through your own effort, will just take care of themselves.

Responsibility

Here is the first and most important step, something you need to take along on this journey: *responsibility*. In my experience, this statement is a little controversial. I hear two reactions quite often.

First: "Of course I am responsible, I am the CEO. What do you imply?" Or, the second: "Why is it my responsibility? I show up, every day, and do my very best. Isn't it the employees' responsibility to *also* show up, give their absolute best with a great attitude, collaborate, innovate, and generally be awesome?"

Let's go back to our garden. Is it the plant's responsibility to grow? Rather, it is in their nature to grow. This is what they do. It is the gardener's responsibility to create an *amazing garden*, with the best conditions for the plants *to thrive*. Just like that, it is your job to create what you wish for in your company. Actually, in a way, this is what you're doing all along: creating conditions for people to work. Yet if it is ineffective, blaming people for it is like blaming the plants in the garden. It doesn't make sense, and it will bring nothing.

Chances are, the conditions you created weren't optimal. We see this in the most of the companies around the world. The management practices that became "normal" were created on assumptions that are not true for most of the people employed. That is akin to planting an apple tree in the desert. The conditions, even if intentional, will not be conducive to *success*. You need to take into account the actual nature and quality of the human being, and then adapt your garden accordingly.

What does this mean to you within the company? Are you "to blame" for all that is not working? No – it doesn't mean that. Assigning blame is a useless exercise. Taking responsibility means committing to improve the situation, committing to solving the problem(s) that you are facing right now, committing to make the future better. This is the first step for everybody in your company, showing up as superstars. Your commitment is to bring them forth.

Reality

The second step is to acknowledge your reality. If your metaphorical car is broken down in the woods, your company is not where you want it to be. Before you initiate any change, you need to fully acknowledge what happens in your company right now. What are its norms? You now have a new lens, a new tool with which to see what is not working. We discussed in the previous chapter that the most widely accepted premises that shape management and the world of work were: "People are lazy, immature, irresponsible profiteers," and, "People are only working for the money." But now we know that those premises are simply not true.

Let's turn them around. Now your new premises will be, "People are good, responsible, caring adults." And, "Everybody wants to contribute and bring forth their biggest talent." These new premises are like magic eyeglasses that will allow you to look at how people are managed in your company, and spot what is not working in that new light. You will ask questions such as, "If my people are responsible, good, competent adults that I trust, why do we have so many obligatory meetings?" Another might be, "If people are good, responsible, caring adults, why don't they trust each other?"

The purpose of this exercise is to see, with greater clarity, how much of your company right now is based on the old premises. It is like a diagnostic tool. Understanding this is fundamental. The key is also to refrain from jumping back into the old frame of thinking, even if it is very convenient, because it is what you know so well. Don't answer the question, *Why are all the meetings obligatory?* with "Because otherwise nobody will show up, because they don't care." You will be tempted to do so, because that is the thinking that we know best. It is easy, familiar, and convenient to default to that mindset, even if it is not right.

That kind of answer would actually block you from progressing, because it keeps you trapped in old thinking and gives you no new information. Look around you, and ask what it is that is not working right now. Would that thing be done differently if we all trusted each other, spoke openly, and assumed the best about each other?

There is another really important question to ask at the outset: "What is working greatly, and what is the story of that? What are the conditions that made that success story possible? Here is a bonus question: "What is *my* contribution to this – both the problems and successes?" Peter Block, in his great book, *The Answer to How Is Yes*, proposes to stop asking: "How do I get those people to change?" Instead, ask: "What is my contribution to the problem I am concerned with?" Just looking around you for a couple of days or hours should give you many possible answers to these questions.

The clarity you will get through asking these questions, from the perspective of the new premises, is priceless. To keep yourself focused during this personal inquiry, I recommend that you keep a journal and make note of your observations for about a week. No need, just yet, to start any big initiatives and involve any other people. Already, through the process of changing your perspective, you will notice changes happening around you. For right now, concentrate simply on your own thoughts, feelings, and observations.

Limiting Beliefs

Before we go any further, we need to look at how most people sabotage themselves already in this phase. You will find that many doubts will come up and make you hesitate. Again and again, the statements I hear from my clients in the beginning sound like:

"This cannot possibly work."

"I cannot trust people with *hard* decisions."

"I feel stupid (or vulnerable) if I trust this guy straight out. I trust him if he will prove it to me that he is trustworthy."

"Look at that guy, he doesn't care a tiny bit."

"That manager is obviously preferring some people over others, and makes life hard for some of his colleagues. He's a jerk. How can he be a good person?"

"Okay, if I trust everybody, and everybody is great and responsible, does it mean that everybody does what they want, and no one else should be able to tell others what to do?"

On and on. Many, many questions. These thoughts will, of course, make total sense to you. If you take them as absolute truth and the only truth possible, they will stop and sabotage your efforts, so be vigilant to their shadows and echoes in your thinking. (For now, simply take note of how they show up also in the dialogue of your management team.)

How can you loosen the grip of such fear-based thoughts and see a clearer, more thoughtful and truthful picture? With my clients, I use a method inspired by The Work™ of Byron Katie to help them overcome their limiting beliefs and see a more complete truth about their situation(s).

Here is how it works: Write down all the thoughts that are tormenting you. Now, take the first one from your list, and write it on the top of a sheet of paper. Don't try to make it nice or more politically correct. This is just for you, so be honest and complete.

Now, you want to validate whether this thought, this statement, is indeed the kind of truth that should serve as the basis of your decisions. For this test, you have to answer four questions about it.

Is it true?

Do you know without a shadow of doubt that it is *always* true? Can you think of any instance when this was *not* true?

How do you feel, and how do you act, when you believe this thought?

Who would you be *without* this thought?

Finally, turn the statement around. What would the opposite of that thought, of that statement, actually look like in practice? There could be several possibilities here. Look at it and ask yourself the question, could the opposite of this statement also be true? Give yourself some time to reflect on the answers.

I use this exercise all the time with my clients and if done rigorously, it will help you loosen the grip of the thoughts that scare and sabotage you and are not necessarily true.

Here is an example of what that could look in practice. Let's take the first thought on my list: "I cannot trust Paul with hard decisions."

I will start by clarifying my thought. *Why can I not trust Paul with hard decisions?* One possible answer is "Paul is not trustworthy." Now let us inquire into this.

Q: Is it true that Paul is not trustworthy?

A: Yes, he once has betrayed my trust by sharing some information I gave him in confidence.

Q: Is this always true?

A: No. Not always. It happened once. On all other interactions, Paul was trustworthy.

Q: How do I feel behave when I believe this thought, that "Paul is not trustworthy"?

A: I feel anger and disappointment. I don't trust him. I am reluctant to share with him not only secrets, but even non-confidential information, because I suspect he will use information to his advantage. I will exclude him from staffing my priority projects. I complain about him. I don't like to work with him.

Q: Who would I be without the thought "Paul is not trustworthy"?

A: I'd be much more relaxed. We'd have a much better relationship. I would be happy for him to be assigned on some projects where he is very well-qualified. He, and the company, could use his expertise so much better.

Now, to the next step. What could be the opposite of the thought "Paul is not trustworthy"?

It could be "Paul is trustworthy," or it could also be, "I am not trustworthy." Let us reflect for a moment on those statements. Could it be that they are *also* true? At times, just as the statement "Paul is not trustworthy" was true that one time. Chances are, if we are truly honest, that we'll find situations where those opposite statements are also true. What does this all mean? It means that often, we hold only one aspect of a complex picture in our minds, and we treat that observation or learning as a complete and entire truth.

"Paul is trustworthy" is not less true than "Paul is not trustworthy," yet we are giving attention and energy to just one part of the truth – and that has undesirable consequences. I am not proposing to completely dismiss your experience. That would not be possible or desirable. I propose to enlarge your experience, so that your feelings and behaviors are not limited by a very narrow perspective that is based on fear. Now, when you encounter Paul, you will always have both thoughts in the back of your mind, as supported by evidence. By dropping your limiting beliefs, you will be able to drop the stories that prevent you from connecting sincerely with people.

Dealing with your limiting beliefs, the ones that keep you from progressing, is an essential part of your foundational work. It is a great part of embracing your power.

You can journal the answer to the questions. Most people find it easier and more effective to work through them with a partner or coach, who can keep them focused on the questions, and witness their inquiry. Use this method to examine all the thoughts and the beliefs that sabotage you, and keep you a prisoner of the old premises: "People are lazy, irresponsibl,e and uncaring," and, "People can only be interested in work through monetary incentive."

Finding Your Ground

This internal work that we just initiated is an essential part of transforming your company. You can think of it as becoming the Batman that is worthy of driving an amazing Batmobile and being part of the Superhero Fleet. While mostly it's exhilarating and interesting, sometimes it can be unsettling. It's almost like when you are between worlds, you have seen that the old one is not working, you know that you need to summon your superpowers, and those of your people, too. But you have no convincing evidence (yet) that it will work in your case.

You have to believe, and to trust, that it will work. That takes courage. We all have within us a well of clarity, courage, and wisdom – but often it is buried beneath the chatter and noise of our everyday, busy lives. In this process, it is essential that you access that well, that source of wisdom at your center. There are many ways, and they all have to do with practices that silence the busy mind, and being mindful of your body and environment. What is the right practice for you? It could be meditation, prayer, any spiritual practice, yoga, sports, or gardening. Anything that interests you, and in the process, clears your mind of chatter. Many people I talk to have such practices already, but many will also tell me that they have "no time" for such things. That mostly means they don't think such activities are important enough to invest the 15 minutes or half hour per day to do them regularly.

Yet we know from research, and I confirm that with my experience with clients, that creating and maintaining a practice that grounds you and connects you with your body, the gateway to your intuition and highest wisdom, is an essential part of your success. Beyond the transformation that you are envisioning for your company, such a practice will also have an amazing impact on all areas of your life. Relationships with the people who matter most to you, health, and peace of mind, will all be enriched through this practice. Finding your ground and training your perspective are also important preparation for times when it won't be easy. Bringing a new way of being and doing your work will challenge some people, and disturb others, even if most people will love it. Your job, in this situation, will be to stand your ground and show flexibility and understanding without compromising on the basic premises.

If you are not prepared for that, initiating change and then jumping back into old patterns will do more harm than good. With the way most companies function today, there is no space to be fully human. We are invited to work to leverage a very small set of skills for a very limited performance, to play a very specific role in a game, with arbitrary and archaic rules, and arcane power plays. It's not really surprising, then, that the world of work is not working. By finding your ground, and dropping your limiting beliefs and stories, you will have the power to set a simpler, saner, more intelligent way of working. When asked for advice, Jean Francois Zobrist, the former CEO of FAVI, would sum it up in two words: "*demerdez-vous.*" This is French, loosely translated, for "un-bullshit yourself" (and your company).

The New Work of the CEO

So what *is* the work of the superhero CEO? Contrary to the popular belief about superheroes, your job will *not* be to be the smartest, strongest. or fastest resource on the team. It is, in this respect, a paradoxical superpower – because it turns the image of the superhero CEO on its head. The popular image of the lonely leader at the top, who knows best in every situation and makes all the heroic decisions, is outdated. Your superpower is precisely to incubate and engage the talents and intelligences of your people – and then let them pour it into the work. As such, it's an amazing capability – but it doesn't place you above them. You are rather working together in the service of each other, and of the goals you set up to achieve.

This work of the CEO is very important: holding the space for people to do their work, but without you having to pretend to have all the answers, or that you have it all figured out to the last detail. To hold that space with intention and full trust, without letting your fear and your ego in the way. We can do that by managing our own fears and, in so doing, creating a safe space for others.

In practice, that means that in the future you might not do some of the tasks you have been busy with until now. Many meetings might become unnecessary, many decisions and authorities over how things are handled might be fully delegated to other people. You might have less work managing conflict, much less bureaucracy, simplified indicators, less data but more meaningful reporting. Here are the essential parts of your work as the CEO:

☐ Holding the space for change and growth.

☐ Initiate and support the change.

☐ Model the new culture.

This formulation and these terms may sound unfamiliar to you, so let me explain.

Hold the Space

Don't let yourself become turned off by this slightly esoteric-sounding title. Holding that space is something you do every day, if you are – for example – a parent. It simply means that you create a safe and intentional environment for your child to learn and grow. This space has several characteristics: safety, trust, and intention. Safety does not refer just to the physical space, or to physical safety, but also to the psychological and emotional kind.

In the case of your child, you want the child to not just be physically safe but also to *feel* safe. For example, by checking for monsters under the bed, by not betraying their trust, by not withholding love, and by not threatening with being thrown out of the house if the child makes a mistake. The same applies for your holding space within your company. We can only give our best, as human beings, if we feel safe. Why? Because humans are not computers, and giving our best implies trying, improving, experimenting, learning, and applying what we have learned. That means that we will also sometimes fail, explore dead-ends, and take missteps. If the space feels safe, those failures will just be a reminder of how many more successes you have once you've internalized the lessons. They will become your best sources of learning and development. Of course, it doesn't work that way in most companies. By declaring and waging a holy war against mistakes and failures, we assure that this space does not feel safe for human beings anymore.

How do people react to that? (Clue: pretty much like children do!) First, they will limit their creative and innovative ideas, abandon experimentation, and only do that in which they can't fail. Second, when mistakes and failure happen (as they will always do), they will try to hide them, cover them up. That makes total sense when people don't feel safe, so it will be very hard to learn from these mistakes or failed initiatives. Instead of making less of it, we will repeat it over and over.

This kind of lack of psychological safety is very common in companies. What happens then, if somebody is abusing this trust, you may ask. The answer is very simple in case of intentional abuse: of course there should be consequences for the abusive person. That shouldn't also mean withdrawing the quality of safety from the entire team or from the entire company, just because one delinquent pushed the limit. As I mentioned, in every group of people, there might be a very small percentage of people who will abuse the space of safety. You will have to resist the urge to turn to police or punish your entire staff all the time because of this isolated incident.

The safety aspect is also connected to the second quality of this space: trust.

Trust refers to many things: trust that the people are inherently good and they hold good intentions; trust that you are doing the right thing; trust in the fact that you and your team have the capacity to find solutions for whatever problems will stand between you and your goal on your way to success. Trust that the people you have hired have the competence and capacity to act as adults, take responsibility, and organize themselves in the best way. Trust, just like safety, is an absolutely essential ingredient. The analogy with being a parent works here, too: if you trust that your child can develop and learn in a certain way, that trust alone will give the child the confidence they need to work towards a goal, even if it is not easy. Our trust will give the child assurance that all is as it's supposed to be, even when they encounter obstacles, and that they are competent, or they can become competent.

The same is true in your company. When people can work in a space of safety and trust, they can create their best work, attain the most cooperation, and achieve mastery. In a space of fear and lack of trust, only very few will ever get close to that.

But how to trust? Some of my clients struggle with that. I hear: "I will trust them when they prove to me that they are trustworthy," or, "I will trust the ones who have been proven, but not the other ones." While holding such thoughts, these clients expect the people working for the company to trust *them* – but it doesn't work that way. One of you will have to trust first, even if there are no 100% guarantees available that you won't be disappointed. Know, however, that experience and science shows that you will be richly rewarded and seldom disappointed when you choose to err on the side of trust.

Trying to save ourselves from disappointment and failure by instituting more and more measurements and indicators and controls is actually counterproductive. I am not saying there should not be controls or checklists or indicators at all. But in most companies there are way too many, and only a small percentage of them are useful. In a space of trust, you and your people can decide what brings value, and can drop the ones that are only there because we don't trust each other.

The third quality of the space is intention. As a company you are coming together to achieve a vision, to be of service. Keeping the highest vision in mind and the possibility of achieving it, that is the intention. You will create and hold an intentional space, a space with a purpose.

How do we actually do it? How do you create that space? Well, as a CEO you are already doing it. You are the holder of the biggest vision of the company, and people are stepping into your space when they step into the company.

Your job is now to make sure that this space has the qualities as I just described. Safety, trust, and intention are required so that people can step up into that space and share it with you. Now, here is the secret about what kind of space that is. The quality of the space itself depends on the inner state of the person holding it. This is very important, so let me repeat it: *The quality of the space you create depends on your inner state.* If you are stressed, if you are tired, or if you don't really like the people you work with, that will show up even when you say all the right words. People will notice and react to that. If you don't trust, if you are nervous, that will be the quality of the space. It is that energy that matters, even beyond the words. This entire chapter is so fundamental, because your beliefs, your values, and your grounding will all determine the quality of the space you create for your company.

You simply cannot fake this. Indeed, it has worked like this up until this point, too, but now you can be much more deliberate and intentional about it – and you can align this space with your vision. You know for a fact that the company will evolve into the direction that you wish for.

Initiating the Change

The process of *demerdez-vous,* of "un-bullshitting" your company – which means moving to a way of working that reflects the new basic assumptions – is best done with lots of sensitivity. Even if it will have dramatic results, the best place for you to initiate it is to start small. Organizations are complex.

This is a case where the car analogy that I used before doesn't work. A car is a complicated machine, made up of many small pieces. But with a good plan and enough engineering knowledge, we can build it together and make it work.

An organization, like your company, is very different. It is a complex system, with many morphing, moving parts. If you move one part, you cannot predict all the consequences of that. The entire system will slightly shift.

Frederic Laloux compares this process in his book, *Reinventing Organizations,* with untangling a ball of spaghetti. Just imagine a ball of spaghetti in front of you. How would you go about the task of detangling it?

Probably the best way would be to observe it first, then to start carefully pulling one spaghetti strand. Gradually, you would observe what happened: did it work? Is it easy? If not, you might look for a different spaghetti strand to pull, or for a way to disentangle a node. Careful, continuous observation here is key. Every move will affect the entire system. It is not like you can make a plan from the beginning to the end, and then blindly execute. After every careful move, you look at the entire system, and determine the best way to proceed. Your job here is to listen and delve into what is the next best step. To listen to people initiate and hold the right conversations, support them, observe them, and then listen again.

In the next chapter, we will talk more about exactly how you listen and how you can initiate the transformation you want. For right now, I just want to underline that this careful and holistic prompting of movement in the company is one of your most important superpowers as the CEO.

Modelling the Culture

This is closely related to holding the space. Your work is to show your people the assumptions and values you hold, and the behaviors you appreciate in practice. In the next chapter, I will explore in detail how you can create a lab, a Sandbox environment for the new way of working that will also work as a model for the rest of the company.

For now, remember that people are looking to you to see how the words that you say translate in practice. How they see you behave is even more important than the words. This is why many CEOs are seen as cynical, insincere, and untrustworthy when they talk about values. These values are obviously not translated anywhere in the company except in the value statement on the wall or on the website. You know better than that, so in the next chapters, I will show you several proven ways to initiate the transformation in your company.

Who Is Holding You?

This chapter was about the fundamental internal work you need to do to be the kind of CEO worthy of the superhero fleet. You will claim your power by committing to transform your ailing management model into a multi-intelligent vehicle of the future.

You will start seeing clearly how the old way of assumptions determines your way of working and managing the company, and you will learn to see the possibilities that will arise when you shift them. You will learn to liberate yourself from the beliefs that limit your capability and potential as a company. You will learn to find your center and strength, a personal practice that will link you to the well of wisdom and peace within you. That will prepare you for your real work as a leader, creating and holding space, initiating and incubating the transformation, and modeling the culture that you want to see.

Can you do this alone? You most certainly can. There are examples of CEOs who went through this transformation alone. It takes, however, a lot of focus, conviction, and determination.

Everything around you is organized and functioning according to the old principles. It is very easy to get busy, distracted, and insecure on this journey. Experience shows that you will have a much better chance for success if you don't walk this journey alone. You are transforming your company in a way that will eventually support your new principles and ideas. But in the beginning, I recommend that you get other kinds of support. That support can come in many forms. It can be a coach, a friend, a colleague from the company, or a connection from outside. The most important thing is that this person understands what you are trying to achieve, supports it, and has the skill and capacity to hold a safe space for you as you are doing your own transformational work.

You are about to create a new world of work in your company. You deserve to be held and supported as you're doing it. Also, it will be easier for you to start studying and modeling this new world if you have somebody supportive who can hold up a mirror and can act as a sounding board for you as issues arise.

A CHANGE
INCUBATOR

*Suddenly, heretics, troublemakers, and change agents aren't
merely thorns in our side – they are the keys to our success.*
–Seth Godin, *Tribes*

* * *

can hardly contain my excitement, because we have arrived
at a point in your journey that will feature some of the best
conversations you've ever had, ground-breaking discoveries
for your company, and the kind of playful joy that will remind
you of your favorite hobby or the time on the playground when
you were six. Until now, it was all about sharpening your view

and preparing your mind. At last, you are ready to get other people on board for this adventure. You are about to bring connection, humanity, joy, meaning, beauty, and (drum roll…) *love* to your work. Your life will be forever richer by experiencing these elements in such abundance. Yes, you will also take your company to and beyond your most ambitious goals, but trust me, this is just the byproduct of being on this amazing journey with your superhero crew.

In the next three chapters, I will show you the step-by-step technology for doing this. Think of it as art. Take painting, as we trained your eye and got rid of your inner blocks in the previous chapter. In this one, you will learn all about technique. What you need to add in abundance is *you* –as in, your presence, and your heart. The only way to do this "wrong" is to go through the movements without really wanting to be there, or without caring. People notice that insincerity. Nobody wants to play with that kid. But if you really want this, I am going to show you how. We set up the playground, the crazy scientist lab, and invite the kids. Be prepared to have your mind blown.

Until now, you have observed and studied your company. That is of course important and fascinating – but not enough for your purposes. Now, we move on to start the transformation in your company. Does this mean that you are finished with the internal work we talked about in the previous chapter? Definitely not. That is a work in progress, and will continue to be. Those practices will serve you well at every step of this process, not only in your work, but also in other areas of life.

For transforming your company, you will have to get as many people as possible to share the new basic assumptions, and share the vision for the management model that supports self-organization, wholeness, and evolutionary purpose. Of course, if this approach is new to your company, you can expect that people will not get on board or even understand right away. It runs against much of the conventional wisdom. Not surprisingly, even those people who will be excited will have their own limiting beliefs and self-sabotaging thoughts that arise in the process. Remember that "de-entangling the spaghetti bowl" metaphor from the previous chapter? That is a good metaphor for how to proceed. In this chapter, I will show you exactly how to do that.

Before we move on to recommendations, I want to define more of what I definitely don't endorse at the outset. I do not recommend trying to change the company from one day to the other by executive decision or copying successful practices from other companies. To be sure, there are CEOs who have done that very successfully (the changing part, not the copying), but it's a radical change. If your people don't get a say in the matter, you will have to deal with a strong, negative backlash and many fears (also, potentially, several people leaving your company at once). To hold space for transformation by force is very difficult. It has been done. Some of the pioneers of this work have changed their companies radically from one day to the other, but it takes enormous courage and tends to be quite traumatic for the company, even when it eventually works out.

A more stable rate of change comes in three phases:

☐ Creating a small core group that will help you hold the entire process.

☐ Creating a Sandbox: a larger group of people who will help shift the thinking in the entire company.

☐ Creating and adopting new practices for the entire company.

In this chapter, I'll show you how to implement phases 1 and 2. The following chapter is dedicated to the third phase.

The Core Group

Who is a member of the core group, and what is its purpose? It is you, and two or three other people who will join you early on in your dedicated journey of transformation. They are the first people who totally get what you are trying to do. If they don't, they are not the right people to be in this group. Among all the qualities you need, the first is to connect to this vision and the new premises upon which you want to build the management model of your company. These others are not necessarily senior managers, or members of the board of directors. Actually, it would be great if at least one or two of them would *not* be. Sometimes, there are people that we think would be really "important" to participate in this. However, when invited, you discover that they are not as excited or curious as you are. That is not a problem. Simply accept that they are, at least this time, not the right people for that role, and invite other people instead.

The most important quality of the people in the core group is that they are open to new approaches and that they care about the company.

Also, this group is not fixed in composition forever. Over time, some people will leave and others will join. You will know when it is right to expand or rotate the team. Right now, at the beginning, you need those who feel excited and intrigued about the possibilities.

Here you might ask me, "Why do I need such a thing? Can I not initiate the larger transformational program right away, on my own?" Several reasons:

Coherence: You want to take the organization to a new level of self-organization, collaboration, and general awesomeness. By now, you know that the key to this is to change the old "command and control" management style. But if you do that by pushing (aka: commanding) people into it, it will feel false, and not authentic or supported, right from the beginning.

People notice and feel such lack of consistency very quickly, and the entire idea loses credibility. With the core group, you have a small "community" in which you can start applying the new premises and the new behaviors that result from them. It is the future you want to see articulated in miniature. That will become a great attractor to the larger community (the rest of your company). I often say to my clients, "It takes a community to hold a community." Your core group will hold the larger community of your company.

Credibility: The people in the core group will be the ones reaching out and inviting people in the next phase (the Sandbox). You will sign the invitations together; you will step up and support the meetings together. If that group has people from various parts and levels of the company, that will create immediate excitement, interest, and (some advance) trust.

Last, but not least, **support.** You can trust the fact that the group will make the entire process better. They will spot inconsistencies, have good ideas, and be a great source of help in organizing sessions. It's not like you can step out of this yet, but it will make your experience much better and enjoyable.

Once you have identified whom to invite, be very deliberate about how you invite them. I'm not exaggerating. The way you approach them is representative of what they can expect if they join.

Start with the Invitation

How do you invite people to a meeting? If you are like most companies, you probably send out an Outlook invitation or similar, maybe with a short agenda. Very often, we don't even say hello in the initial email, which is just as well, because most people won't read it. This is more a notification than an invitation, and it is so widespread and taken for granted that most people don't ever question it. But you are doing something new here. You want to initiate a process in your company that will result in healing the systemic lack of trust, and then in bringing people together in a new way. You want your people to show up with openness, curiosity, and excitement. You want to set the intention and the tone of the conversation already, before it starts. This is part of you preparing a space for it. This is why you need to invite your new team in a different way than usual.

The new way has to reflect your new intentions and premises. Think about a time when you got an invitation that captured your imagination, an invitation that made you really curious and intrigued. What made that invitation exciting? I will venture to say that it was probably an invitation that made you feel like you are seen and you matter. It's a beautiful invitation. Maybe it was an invitation that promised genuine connection, friendship, and fun. Maybe it was an invitation that honored your professional achievement, connected you with other passionate people in your organization, and beyond. You got the sense from that invitation that your presence is valued and your time and effort was honored.

Also, most probably, you weren't forced to go.

You want to create your invitation in this spirit. At the beginning, you will invite a few people to be part of your core group. Reach out and invite your core group people in personal conversation, not through email.

Preserve Their Freedom

Getting an invitation from the CEO may feel, in many companies, like it is compulsory and sometimes intimidating. Think about the best way to talk to this person so that they feel valued, respected, and not talked down to. Maybe the best place is in a café or in the sofa corner of a meeting room, maybe by the fireplace—less formal, more open space. You want to place yourself on equal footing for this conversation, and not dominate it from above.

Share Your Vision

Share your vision and your thoughts, and ask for your core people to join you so you can do this together. You have to make it very clear that there are absolutely no consequences for them saying *no*. Also, you have to put your money where your mouth is, and make it clear that you will have their back if and when this might lead to more work hours, which might sometimes be the case.

Share Your Questions

At this point, you are just convening the first people for your movement. The people who will answer your call now will be your biggest supporters. You don't need to show up like you have figured out every single detail, like you know exactly what the future looks like (because you don't!).

Commit to Figuring it out Together

At every step in this process, you might be tempted to show that you know exactly how this will look and that you have an answer to all possible questions. That would be dangerous. There are no fail-proof blueprints, only paths to walk on and journeys to take towards your goals.

Share Your Own Inspiration

This is also the right time to share some of the example resources that have inspired you. Ask the group for their vision for the company and listen deeply. The purpose of this conversation is to get two or three people from the company to share your excitement and help you invite in the next group that is a little larger.

Listen!

This is also a place to listen deeply to the thoughts of the people you invite. Know that, no matter what they say, their reaction is representative of the thinking of others, too. Honor them by letting them know that you hear them, and that you value their input.

Your next move is to meet with this little group several times. The purpose of these meetings is to get to know each other, to build trust, to share inspiring stories from the company and beyond, to support each other as you are pushing through limiting beliefs, and to explore what would be possible if everybody shared the new basic premises, and if people worked in your company all the time as they do in those inspiring stories. Think of it as a think tank, book club, or peer coaching group. You don't have to deliver anything for the first several meetings. The sharing and supporting work that I mentioned is the only deliverable. With these meetings, you are setting up a new field, a space where these ideas live outside of your own head. My clients tend to be a little scared by this at the beginning, but once they start, they find it, without exception, very exciting and affirming.

Once people start to feel safe, as you ensure the confidentiality and safety of the conversation, you will find that it is easy to create common ground on the new premises. Of course, our dominant business culture expects that we have a clear goal, so people might expect that from you. Try to resist that pressure, call your group some crazy name (Batmobile Task Force, anyone?) to give a clear signal that this is a new space with different rules. Also, with this approach, you can better deal with some of the politics that may arise around this, such as certain people feeling slighted, thinking they should have been invited. At this point I advise my clients to reassure whoever asks that everybody will be invited in a couple of weeks, and that this is merely a consultative group that shares case studies.

This is just the beginning. Your group will create its own vision and goals pretty soon, using words that they are meaningful to you all. In my experience, after a couple of meetings, your small group will desire to *do* something. This will be your next step. The next task of this group is bringing together a larger group, some 15 to 30 people. I call this group the Sandbox, because it is both a play and testing ground for the new ideas that arise from the new, shared assumptions.

The Sandbox

This process, as you might have guessed, is iterative. You established trust and shared your vision. Now it is time for your small group, and perhaps yourself, to invite a select number of other people in. Invite people who are well-versed with different parts of your company, because they are natural connectors that will help legitimize the ideas socialized in your core group among the more skeptical employees.

Also, make sure that the group is not dominated by senior management. That would not be healthy for real, open conversation – or for bringing in new ideas. Choose collaborative people who will mesh well with the people in the core group.

Again, invite them by reaching out personally. Divide up the personal conversations between the people in the core group, and then follow up with a written invitation.

Keep in mind everything that we've already said about how to invite. Invest some time in writing the invitation (together with some people in the core group), and then sign it together. It will be much, much more powerful if the people in the core group invite new participants together by signing the invitation, than it would be if any one person invites them alone (even if that one person is the CEO).

You can have different ways of engaging the "Sandbox" people. Each company has its own identity and particularities, and you want to factor that in. I propose you initiate a process that has worked successfully for my clients, and it is one that you can easily adapt to your company.

Schedule a couple of meetings with this new group (max. two weeks apart, two to two-and-a-half hours each). The first meeting is to establish relationships and trust.

The second one is to start the conversation about what it could mean *in practice* for your company to change the old management premises to the new ones.

I will start by teaching you the core principles that make this entire process work, and then I will give you the templates that you can use to structure your meetings.

About Trust

I don't mean to say that it will take you just one meeting to establish everlasting trust with this group, or within your company. No one meeting of any kind can accomplish this. Rather, think of trust as a precious and rare plant that you need to cultivate (again, in your garden, metaphorically speaking) and cannot buy on the market. It will take some time, care, and commitment to grow it. At first, you need to create a little clearing, maybe a hothouse, a space where the conditions are right for the seeds to grow. This is what you do with these meetings. You create a space that functions according to the new rules and the new assumptions that you want to establish. It is a space with no initial purpose other than to experiment with the new assumptions and to grow trust, and not just trust in you – even more importantly, trust in each other.

Your job is to create this clearing and protect it. I sometimes hear from CEOs that the 90-minute meeting every couple of weeks is too much. People don't have time for that. In reality, they don't have time because it is not considered important. If you want to change the fundamental assumptions of "people management" in your company, this will be a priority. You want to make sure that people know it is important and valued by you. Often, those attending the meetings will know that already because of the way you invited them. Their colleagues and superiors may not see the benefits right away, and make it difficult for them to participate. Your job is to protect the people in this meeting, making sure that they are no adverse consequences for their participation. In time, as little as a month or two, you will start seeing the results.

Conversations That Matter

Think about your most formative years. What were the conversations there that touched you most? What were the conversations that created revelations for you? Maybe it was in high school or on a sports team, with a teacher, a coach, a parent. Maybe it was with your best friend, or maybe it was as a college student debating the meaning of life at 2 a.m. in a bar. The engrossing conversations where you felt a deep connection with the people around the table where you could share what really mattered to you and what questions didn't let you sleep at night, where you could ask and listen deeply. You knew that you mattered to those around the table, and that you could show up in all your glory and splendor, and with all your insecurity and doubts, because you knew that this was not about power games – it was about what deeply mattered to you. Those are conversations that shape who we are, what we believe, and what we in turn will create in our lives. In a traditional corporate culture, there is no place for such conversations.

First of all, there is no trust. Then there is no time. And finally, there is no point. These aren't conversations that you can create around a tight agenda with clear deliverables. They're not efficient, so clearly, why bother? You want to bring such conversations back, conversations that have the quality of deeply impacting us, that speak to the questions that bother us, conversations based on trust where we can show up and bring all our gifts.

In a traditional corporate culture based on fear and lack of trust, you cannot have those conversations, but in your new core group and Sandbox group, they're an essential tool. Now to be sure, those conversations from the good old days were based on relationships of trust forged over time. They developed organically. Wouldn't it be great if you would have a magic wand or a superpower to create such amazing, transformative conversations at any time with just about anybody? Good news: you have this capacity, and I am going to show you exactly how to access it.

The Art and Science of Meaningful Conversations

The quality of a conversation is set already before anybody is in the room. This is because people come into a meeting with a clear set of expectations and assumptions. The usual corporate expectations and assumptions will not lead to a meaningful transformative conversation. The quality is set the moment you are starting to think about the meeting and the conversation.

Intention

What is your intention with this? What is the greatest thing, the highest goal that could be achieved by people having a genuine exchange about questions that truly matters to them and to the company? If you answer that, you'll know that this will be your intention for the meeting. Your job is to keep this intention at the center, as everything you will do around this meeting will serve that purpose.

Invite with Intention

We spoke already about invitation. The language of the invitation, whether spoken or written, will need to reflect your intention for the conversation, as well as the kind of space you will create for it, in an atmosphere of trust and integrity. When you are starting out and reaching out to the first people, it will be you alone doing the inviting. As soon as you have your first mate in your core group and reach out to the subsequent group, the Sandbox, start signing the invitations together. Have at least two people collaborating on the invitation and then have it signed by everybody.

This might sound cumbersome and time-consuming, but these are special meetings, and you will be amazed by the quality of the response and the ownership that you'll experience.

Hold Space for Trust, Potential, and Integrity

We have spoken before about holding space. It is what you do for your company and in particular for every conversation. With the mental preparation I described in the previous chapter, you will open and hold a space of trust, potential, and integrity. That will create almost instant trust, and the feeling of connection that is fundamental for a meaningful conversation.

Physical Space

The space where you hold your meetings and conversations has a great effect on how people feel, and how they engage with each other. Many of our traditional meeting rooms are set up in a way that might encourage an intellectual debate, but effectively discourage emotion, and, therefore, really engaging with each other. They are sterile, bare, functional rooms with no soul: hard seats, a table in the middle taking up most of the space, separating people from each other. People slump up to their shoulders under the table, and flee into their phones. Sometimes there is no natural light. People mostly gather to look at papers or PowerPoint presentations, but not to look at each other. The energy present is most often such that people cannot wait to leave as soon as they can.

Sometimes we have the possibility to completely change the space. Sometimes, we can simply rearrange it a little. I often move the tables out, and just leave a circle of chairs or sofas with some beautiful centerpiece, e.g., flowers or stones, something that brings the presence of nature into the room. I make sure that there is enough light and air in the room. I try to avoid presentations in order to concentrate on seeing and listening to each other. If it is possible, I offer some nice, healthy snacks and drinks. Breaking bread with each other is an intimate experience that builds relationship like no other.

These are small things, but intentionally setting up the space for your conversation is a powerful gesture that will take you a long way towards success.

Craft and Ask Powerful Questions

A powerful question is a question that opens our thinking to that next level of possibility. Many questions do not fall in this category, including: questions that are not genuine, e.g., when we already know the answer; rhetorical questions; questions for information ("When do you need the report?"); or yes-no questions ("Do you need help with the report?").

To create a truly powerful question, take the question you already have and see how can you broaden or challenge some of its basic assumptions to open new possibilities. For example, the question: "What new goals should we set?" Imagine that it can become: "What is possible for us to create together?" Even, "What do we need to do, or who do we need to be, to provide the best service to our clients?"

Powerful questions go a level deeper, searching for the impactful question behind our initial (surface) question. Searching for and crafting a powerful question is never a waste of time. With a good question, you will have insights and breakthroughs as a rule – not as an accident. Einstein has famously said: "If I had an hour to solve a problem and my life depended on the solution, I would spend the first 55 minutes determining the proper question to ask, for once I know the proper question, I could solve the problem in less than five minutes."

A powerful question:

- □ is simple and clear;
- □ is thought-provoking;
- □ generates energy;
- □ focuses inquiry;
- □ surfaces unconscious assumptions; and
- □ opens new possibilities.

Powerful questions are among your most important tools. Creating them is something you want to do in advance. The time and the thinking you put in it will be richly rewarded by the quality of input and responses from your people. Also, crafting powerful questions is an art and a practice. It is an important part of the preparation and something I always dedicate time and attention to. The more you do it, the better you will get at it. This skill will serve in all areas of life, especially if you are raising children.

Design for Participation

How do you get people to talk? If the group is larger than six people, you can't rely on spontaneous participation. Some people are more extroverted, more naturally inclined to jump in to contribute on every question and speak at length. In a larger group, this will exclude and alienate many of the quieter types. Sometimes you have a group with people who are on different hierarchical levels in the organization. Some of them are used to being listened to and being shown deference, while others are conditioned to hold back.

These power relations will follow people into the room at first, and they will influence the conversation. But you want to create a space that is liberated of those constraints.

This is why, in order to create a safe space for all voices, you will need to use participatory methods to organize your conversations. I will describe some of the methods I use in chapter 6. For now, just know that especially when you have a larger group, it's essential to structure the conversation in a non-emphatic way, so that everybody feels safe and senses the possibility to contribute constructively.

Harvest with Intention

Harvesting is a word from agriculture, yet I like to use it in this context to illustrate a very different approach to gather and make use of the results from meetings and conversations. Harvesting the results of a conversation means gathering the fruits in a form that is useful going forward.

So I encourage you to stop taking the kind of "meeting minutes" that nobody reads. Instead, think in advance together with your core group, for example, about how would you like to use the results of this meeting. Maybe it will be a list of recommendations, maybe just a photo record of having had a good conversation, and the statement of the breakthroughs achieved. Whatever you decide, it is only important that it be useful. That is going to ensure that your conversation will travel, will live on, and will be useful even beyond the group of the participants who are there.

More importantly, the mere fact that you talk in advance about what form the "harvest" (or the outcome) should take will increase the quality of your work in the group exponentially.

Keep the Integrity

This part is about ensuring safety and trust. When you promise something or you commit to something, you have to actually do it.

If you can't follow through, don't promise, and be very open about it. Also, if you agreed to confidentiality, remind everybody to respect that. A lot of this is obvious, but I find it useful to remind ourselves how easily the trust – and the great spirit of open conversation – can be broken. We are not talking here of only one particular conversation, but also the overarching one happening as you are starting a new age in the life of your company. Trust is the most important ingredient of success. Be the guardian of it.

As promised, I prepared two possible meeting design templates for you. You can download them (free) from: www.theceosplaybook.com

To be sure, there are endless ways to design amazing and productive Sandbox meetings. In chapter 6, I give you an entire toolbox of methods and approaches that you can use to make the Sandbox a true incubator of creativity and collective intelligence in the company.

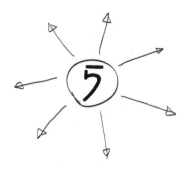

UNLEASH THE
BRILLIANCE
(OF YOUR TEAM)

B y creating the Sandbox group, you just created the engine for innovation and new management. That engine is going to deliver not only new ideas, but also great engagement in your company. You started by inviting some people to the meetings, but of course, you can rest assured that everybody will know about it pretty fast. During the first three months, I recommend that you keep meetings mostly to the group you invited initially, so that this habit of conversation has time to strengthen. After this time, extend the invitation.

If your company is made up of less than 70 people, invite everybody who wants to come. A great question to discuss in your Sandbox group is precisely: "How to extend the invitation to the rest of the company?" You want to make sure that nobody feels forced to attend. There is no unspoken expectation that they should participate.

If your company is larger, I would let people in the Sandbox invite their friends, people whom they think would profit from the dialogue and enjoy being part of it. Also, invite anybody who expresses interest to come. This is more of an organic growth, but it is a healthier, more personal way in which this idea, and this way of work, will travel through your company. Ask people to extend the invitation to those who they consider appropriate. It has a way of working out so that you will always get the right people in the room.

You can cut the number of attendees to a maximum of 50, especially if you don't know how to facilitate large group conversations effectively.

The Sandbox will be a place where people will bring up burning issues related both to work and to management. Also, this will be a place for ideas, discoveries, and revelations. Your people will leave inspired to act, to implement their ideas. This is the moment when the new management culture, based on the new premises, meets for the first time with the old management culture in the field. You will have two paradigms facing each other. The goal is clear: bringing as much of the new thinking and values in as possible, while preserving what works well from the old system.

What Kinds of New Ideas?

You will have all sorts of new ideas and possible solutions coming from the conversations in the Sandbox group. They will come as answers to the burning questions your people will ask. Very often, especially at the beginning, they will have a great need to ask many questions and share, just because they finally can. Sometimes, the question will be easy to answer or to solve. Sometimes, the mere fact of asking the question will highlight for everybody the need to have a deeper conversation. As an example, people in the company of one my clients asked, for the first time, to receive a printout of their salary calculations every month, not only an electronic version. This was a very simple request that was easy to satisfy, yet for the people involved, it was a top priority. The CEO of the company was even wondering why people have not simply asked for this before. Indeed, it is very typical that such a request can be made more easily when people feel appreciated and encouraged to ask.

As a CEO, you often don't have an accurate perspective from above if the culture in your company encourages or discourages such questioning. In the case I just mentioned, the CEO thought that the employees could have asked for this any time as a matter of course. The real measure of the culture is not the way the CEO feels about something, but how the employees perceive he or she might. Such simple requests for improvement were great eye-openers for how the employees felt regarding their safety and tenure in everyday life within the company. Other burning issues in the same company concerned (in the example that I mentioned) staff rotation, under-staffing, and creating better ways to rearrange the technical equipment.

In the first such conversation, it was like a lid had been blown off. People felt a great urge to give their feedback to the CEO and demand solutions, but during that session, the CEO did not become defensive, try to look all-knowing, or solve all the problems. She did take note of some suggestions that were clear, simple, and straightforward, and she acted on them promptly. But some of the issues raised were not so easy and obvious to solve. In subsequent meetings, people started contributing constructive ideas or solutions to their own burning questions. What the CEO had to do here was to keep convening the group, keep reassuring them that it was safe to ask questions, have them improve their questions, and seek constructive solutions.

Ideas for Work Improvement

Often, this group will either come up with new solutions or encourage a conversation, beyond this group, that will result in some kind of proposal. Keep an eye on the journey of such proposals, as they can highlight both remarkable strengths and great dysfunctionalities in your company. It can be, for instance, that such initiatives are systematically killed or stalled because they are "not coming from the right people," in which case you have highlighted a significant systemic problem in your company. This is a typical old-style management or old-premises issue that will clash with the more open and participatory approach that you propose and endorse. You can identify these issues by asking people to report back to the group on what happened to their ideas.

Here is another way to support these incentives: Make it clear to the managers in your company that you see this work as a way to increase participation, devolve decision-making (free management from many decisions the people in their teams are competent to make), increase transparency, improve motivation and innovation. You are doing that actively by the work with the core group and the Sandbox, but ideas need to be tested and implemented. You can help open up management to these ideas by showing your support and appreciation for the new initiatives. You can think of it as a way to support strengthening the new premises in your company.

Systemic Improvements

What you created with the Sandbox group, led by the core group, is like a workshop for your vehicle, if we return to use of the vehicle metaphor. At the beginning, people will concentrate on fixing the old vehicle, because this is the only means of travel they know. As they ease into this liberated space of the Sandbox group and experience being together on the new premises, they will be ready to start transforming the old vehicle into the new-style Batmobile that will serve in the new territory.

Here are two questions that can start a great conversation in this direction:

Where is the energy currently blocked or waiting to be set free in our company?

For which kind of change improvement is there more energy?

Both are great questions to be asking of the Sandbox group. These are quite high-level inquiries, so you shouldn't expect direct action coming from them right away, but if you keep holding them, they will soon turn up very specific ideas and initiatives.

Here is gentle and loving advice: At every step of this journey, your faith will be tested. Most of us have been so deeply programmed to mistrust people, that you may well feel somewhat scared about supporting people to believe in their own ideas. In chapter 6, I will introduce you to the Advice Process, which is a repeatable process that you can use to validate the initiatives. But do not judge (openly, and if you can, also be mindful not to in your heart) what people come up with, even if some things sound challenging or misinformed. If you get cold feet at this point and start judging and controlling, then you stand to lose the credibility and trust that you will need to transform your company.

I want to discuss three specific areas where significant change can start:

- ☐ wholeness,
- ☐ self-organization, and
- ☐ evolutionary purpose.

These three areas are where you want to encourage breakthroughs, for these are the hallmarks of truly evolved companies (the research of Frederic Laloux in *Reinventing Organizations* has substantiated this).

Wholeness

Wholeness refers to the capacity of your company to welcome, use, and honor the many talents that people can offer, not just a very narrow set of skills. Also, it refers to a sense of care within a company for the well-being and the health of the employees. A sense of wholeness is essential for the sustainability of the company, providing an environment in which people can feel supported and appreciated; a place where there is a fundamental recognition of the fact that work *is* life, and not *opposed* to life. Something that needs to be balanced out in a constantly shaky life-work balance in today's business cultural norms.

Under the old management premises, wholeness is regarded with deep suspicion. Everything that supports physical and mental health – such as breaks, vacation, telecommuting, parental leave – is seen as a concession, and not an asset to the work. Yet, we know that creating a workspace that supports and completes the other areas and honors other interests in life is a significant asset to the company. Initiatives in this area, such as telecommuting, flexible hours, creating cozy conversation places in the corridor, or offering mindfulness classes during the lunch break by a colleague who has studied it, are often met with resistance by the (old-style) management.

This resistance stems from the suspicion that people will abuse these possibilities and not work as much. This is a great opportunity to exercise your faith in the new premises (the people are good, mature, responsible, and motivated). Let go of the fear. Of course, all the initiatives will be assessed for feasibility, but if the dominant thinking is, "How can we make this work?" and not, "They only want to take advantage of me and we cannot afford such things," then you have already made progress.

Self-Organization

Self-organization and a high degree of autonomy are markers of a company that is not burdened by too many management levels or too many non-productive tasks. The corporate development of the last 50 years, with its strong focus on efficiency and specialization, created many new roles in companies, such as HR, Compliance, all kinds of liaising roles, and so on. That all comes in addition to the management levels (also coordinating and controlling roles). The original thinking behind this high-level specialization is that if people are able to focus only on their area of best expertise, they won't "waste time" on tasks for which they are over- or under-qualified. However, that thinking has backfired spectacularly.

Let's take, for example, the HR department of a company with some 500 employees. Chances are, HR is separate from the core business, and the department spends lots of time divining how to find good people to complement a workplace or a team with which they are not intimately familiar. Or, trying to research (and divine) what kind of training the company should offer, only to arrive, after lots of communication and research at promoting something people don't really care about. In order to survive, this department will try to create and service new needs: training and development, organizational learning, and so on.

I have been a consultant in this field for many years. I can attest that often the result is disjointed departments, where people have forgotten how to do some essential business functions for themselves.

The biggest offender, however, is management. How does it work in your company? Can the people who are the most competent to make a decision actually make them? If you are like the most companies, chances are the answer is no (or a variation of "no"). Instead, management has to be informed and educated, just to make a (not better) decision than a professional more directly involved could easily have made without extra background and review. Companies that give all the decision-making power and the power of proposing developments to the people who are directly involved and impacted have been shown to make better decisions, save money, and have much, much more engaged employees. It is not even a close comparison.

Not surprisingly, increasing people's autonomy and capacity for self-organizing is an area where you should support initiative. The ideas here can be very different. Teams can decide to create their own schedules. Teams might wish to do their own hiring (and only ask for specialized support from the HR department). People might propose to have more control over their budgets, or to have differently allocated budgets (such as a dedicated travel budget). The scope can vary, from reducing the numbers of sign-offs you need to finalize your PowerPoint presentation to complete self-organizing, in which companies have eliminated the managerial levels and all the managerial tasks are delegated to the employees. In some cases, the team even hires or elects their own managers. Needless to say, the more autonomy people have, the more ownership people feel, and the more dedicated they are to the tasks and objectives they carry out every day.

As you start off, chances are that your people will not propose anything so radical. Under the old premises, there was a lot of fear of abuse. Under the new premises, however, this kind of work style only makes sense.

Here is an example of how one such company, Sun Hydraulics, which is a global company employing some 900 people, is talking about their way of working on their careers page:

"If you're looking to be told what to do, Sun is not the place for you. There is no organizational chart or formal job descriptions here. No reserved parking spaces or executive offices.

"What you will find are collaborative people who enjoy their work. These are people whose ever-growing skills and knowledge eclipse the confines of any title. These are curious people who ask tough questions and work with each other to find answers. These are people who know what they're good at and take ownership over the quality of their work: not because they report to someone, but because they're self-directed.

"Sun offers competitive salaries and benefits. We've grown about 20 percent a year, compounded annually, since 1972 and have one of the most comprehensive screw-in hydraulic cartridge and manifold product lines in the world. We have operations in the US, UK, Germany, Korea, France, China and India. And we believe it is employee freedom and flexibility that keeps our turnover low and our growth strong.

"Do you have what it takes to contribute to Sun?"

Evolutionary Purpose

Traditionally, the company strategy – thinking about where it should go next, what products it should try, what new markets it might approach or how it should expand into new demographics –all comes from the head, or the top-tier management. Sometimes the strategy is successful, and sometimes it fails – but truly what happens is that we waste invaluable guidance that people in the company, on every level, could contribute to these decisions. Think about the company as a human body, in which the CEO or senior leadership is the brain that tells the body what it should do. However, the brain is not the only intelligent part, at least not the only part capable of providing feedback and direction. Every cell is a sensor of some sort, and we have experiences of generations coded in our genes, intuition, urges, and needs. Sometimes my brain tells me that everything is fine, yet my body senses tension and danger in my environment. Sometimes my brain tells me to keep working another two hours, yet my body tells me to go to sleep. If my brain ignores my body for too long, I find that I will predictably become ill.

This is what happens to the company, too. The intelligence about how the company should develop, and what could be the next big thing, is distributed among its people. If the company is prepared to listen and integrate this intelligence, its chances of growing and thriving are immensely greater. This is closely related to wholeness and self-organization. If you can make space for people, their complex lives, and their multiple talents (wholeness), and you can guarantee their autonomy and initiative, then the company can truly become a multi-intelligent vehicle with great capacity to adapt.

There are many examples for that. Let me share two with you.

One of the biggest successes ever for Harley-Davidson, the famed motorcycle maker, was the establishment of biker clubs (the Harley Davidson Owners Club). The community created around these biker clubs has turned customers into loyal fans, a tribe so enthusiastic and committed that it has no match. The idea for biker clubs came neither from the CEO nor some strategy task force, but from the workshop floor. It was the idea of a factory worker, however it was because of the leadership of famed CEO Vaughn Beals that this idea was heard and could be implemented. His approach to management was based on precisely the beliefs that people are good, valuable, talented, caring, and responsible. The results were dedicated and happy employees, but also an iconic brand and a huge commercial success.

Another example is the company Gore-Tex. Its founder, Bill Gore, used to work with DuPont (a big multinational chemical company), but left the organization precisely because he felt that his ideas were not taken seriously. In the company he created (Gore-Tex), everybody can propose and implement new products. Bill Gore has established a culture of participation that will create success and live on even after he is gone. It has led to an amazingly wide range of products (ranging from astronaut suits to guitar strings) and sustained success on the market, and has the distinction of consistently ranking among the best employers for decades. Gore-Tex is a great example of all three areas at work: wholeness, self-organization, and evolutionary purpose.

Clash of Systems

We are now at the point where you have created an incubator for new initiatives and ideas, and some of those ideas want to be implemented. Here is what you have to know: conversation in the Sandbox and throughout the company is important and it is also a form of action, but soon people will want to see their everyday work impacted and improved by it. If it doesn't translate into any change, your people will lose their faith in the transformative power and credibility of your new approach. But here is the thing: The old system you had in place does not allow for this kind of insurgency, often even when it comes to harmless proposals that don't not challenge authority and straightforward ideas. Traditional management is designed for survival, and will attack and destroy (pretty much like an immune system would) all that threatens its legitimacy.

Let's say people want more autonomy over their work. As an example, let's say that instead of checking three times back and forth with a manager and colleagues about a project proposal, then waiting for the managers to sign off on it, they want to just check one time and integrate all the feedback the best way they see fit – and then send it off. Such a change can feel threatening to the manager, who will be worried not only about potential mistakes, but even more about losing authority and significance. If checking and giving feedback is how management believes they add value, taking this away is understandably threatening. The managers, like everybody else, have learned to function and perform according to expectations. In the old system, they delivered what they have learned is expected from them and what they know will be rewarded. It is not surprising that a "systemic change," where their job and their success factors are significantly altered, will be hard for some and will likely encounter resistance. While the traditional management system works less and less for most people and for companies as a whole, it still does work for others, mostly middle management, whose function has been defined in relation to it. Your next steps here are to help them find the articulation of their new role, and define their added value in a way that is in alignment with the new premises.

There will be some people who can't do it. For instance, if someone's major motivator and source of identity is exercising power over other people, it might be that they can't take this curve. But for most of managers, this can be a great opportunity to do more of what they love while knowing that their work is truly meaningful. What is happening here is that the old system is slowly dying – not because of the new conversations taking place in your company, not because of your new premises that you want to introduce, or the core group or the Sandbox group and their initiatives – but because the territory has changed. Just as in my metaphor earlier in this book – that broken-down car – the vehicle is not only broken, it is no longer appropriate for the environment in which we find ourselves. The general malaise that we experience about the world of work reflects precisely that.

When the new thing is born, as an alternative to the old, we are tempted to either jump on it and trash the old – or, if the old system has worked for us, trash and attack the new system. Yet the best way to support your company is to honor the old, honor the learning, and acknowledge the fact that people will be grieving for certain aspects of it. Honor that which was, because at one point it also represented progress and innovation. Help people, especially managers, find their place in the new system. In the same space, you support the new – at first by creating a safe environment for incubation and connecting the change makers; later by getting out of the way and letting people do the work.

How to Support the Transition

Transforming the way people are managed and how the work is organized is a fundamental change. You can help them by creating a safe space for them to grieve without enabling them to get stuck in their story. Also, you can help them play an active role in designing the new system and their new role. You will see that those who take this in a hard way will go through the stages of grief (just like in the grieving theory of death and dying expert Elisabeth Kübler-Ross): denial, anger, bargaining, depression, and finally acceptance. Here is how to support them in every stage.

Denial

In this space, you can expect that many people are ready to vehemently deny any need for change and all the thinking behind the new premises. They are not ready to see the opportunities and they easily dismiss any inspiration. This is why it is really important that you provide the safe space for new thinking to develop in the beginning with the call to the Sandbox group.

What can you do? Acknowledge that this is new and that change is challenging. Reaffirm that you see that change is necessary. Help them break through their own limiting beliefs (sometimes I work with small groups through the limiting beliefs questions, from chapter 3).

Anger

Some people will be angry if things don't go their way or if they're overruled, especially if they were used to having the last word. When mistakes are made, as always happens in the new system (just like in the old one), they will blame you, the changes, and everybody else for them.

What can you do? Change does not mean chaos, it does mean, however, that you will have some new rules. Acknowledge and reaffirm the rules, acknowledge responsibility, do not blame. Dealing with conflict and emotions in a team is an important skill that is traditionally the job of the manager. I encourage my clients to strengthen this capacity in their entire staff. The more people in the organization who know how to create a space of safety and confidence, the better.

Bargaining

At this point, people will try to get the best deal for themselves and try to work out special rules that apply only to them.

What can you do? Have them define their new work as managers and help them see the value in it. Chances are, they'll like it more, because there is more meaningful, value-adding work and less paper-pushing and controlling. Help them see that they are at the service of their team, and that the highest service they can give is supporting their team in the way their team needs it. If they do that, they'll gain legitimacy coming from the team, not only from their bosses, and that's much more valuable.

Depression

Some people may suffer from a loss of status, especially if a big part of their work was in micromanaging and controlling.

What can you do? Invite them to be part of the good conversations in the Sandbox group. These are people with valuable knowledge and skills for your company. Give them an opportunity to contribute, and honor their contribution. The Sandbox group conversations are also a great way to get to know people and build relationships with colleagues from many parts of the company.

Acceptance

This is the point when even the skeptics start to appreciate the great possibilities, and even the great potential and beauty, of the new management premises. You can count on some of these former skeptics to be among the greatest fans of this work. Of course nothing will be more convincing and attractive than successes. For that, you need to support the people and the initiatives that are coming from the Sandbox group.

Being Relevant, Being in Service

Here is an exercise that managers can do with their teams to make sure that their work is relevant:

Prepare a list (bullet points) with their top six activities. These may be the activities that are the most important and take up the most time in their workday.

Give this list to the people on their team, and ask them to draw a pie chart indicating how much of their time and energy they think each activity should take up.

The manager will also prepare their own pie chart, with the actual time each activity takes up (as a percentage of total time at work).

Compare the results from the people on the team with the reality of the manager. In my experience, this exercise often shows that the people on the team want more support and "coaching" time with their supervisors, and less control and policing from them. Also, many managers spend a lot of time with the activities of "managing up," that is, building the relationships with their own supervisors. That is also important, but not nearly as important as being there for your team.

The manager can then have a conversation with the team about what kind of support they would like to see more of, and adjust accordingly.

This is a great process to review after a couple of months, and it often brings lots of improvement in the relationships and work of the team.

TOOLBOX

*We can't solve problems by using the same kind of thinking
we used when we created them.*

– Albert Einstein

* * *

This chapter is all about the how. Until now, I told you about what to do, i.e., create a safe space, free of the all limiting and hindering assumptions that created today's failing corporate cultures. First, you created it within yourself, and then you extended it to increasingly larger parts of the company, together with your colleagues. First with just very few people, then a few more, and more. You will now guide and support your people toward a new normal, where the new thinking and management premises are the laws of the land. This is all you need to do.

Your two most important tools for this are:

☐ Your capacity to question the default common wisdom that limits your thinking, and to choose to make your own observations and manage your own mind.

☐ Creating transformative conversations. Think of this conversation as your best, secret super-weapon or, even better, as your magic wand.

These shifts are not, as they are often discounted, just talk. Powerful, intentional conversation at every stage will change the default way of thinking and acting in your company. For everyone.

In the words of Mahatma Gandhi:

"Your beliefs become your thoughts,

Your thoughts become your words,

Your words become your actions,

Your actions become your habits,

Your habits become your values,

Your values become your destiny."

The tools I am going to give you are powerful tools of transformation. I share them with you at this point, because if you got this far in this book, I am confident that you will use them wisely and intentionally – as they are meant to be used. In fact, I have already mentioned some of the tools in the previous chapters. The overcoming limiting beliefs based on inquiry (i.e. The Work™, by Byron Katie), creating new thoughts or crafting and asking powerful questions. (For that, I recommend *The Art of Powerful Questions*, by Juanita Brown).

In the coming pages, I am going to give you some more tools to draw out the creativity in the room, in order to create conditions to tap into people's strengths and talents and help them seek advice and take decisions.

Design

You might wonder why there is a need to plan so carefully – indeed, to design the entire meeting with the core group, the Sandbox group, and eventually with any significant meetings with many people in the company. Preparation is nothing new. It is a normal, expected practice – and a sign of respect for the people attending that the meeting is well-prepared. However, the traditional way of preparing meetings will not lead to any creative input and real participation, not surprisingly, because that was normally not the expected output!

Think about it. Somebody around the table presents something, a document or a PowerPoint slide. Then they ask, "Does anybody have any questions?" Maybe they implore, "Feel free to ask any questions." It's not really inviting. Instead, it sounds like: "I hope you don't have any questions." This is not a real and sincere opening. It does not invite the more fundamental, more creative conversation to take place. Even if you are not looking for great creative contributions, you can always ask a better question that focuses attention and invites answers. Maybe you can ask, "Will this information be useful to me?" How about, "What are the consequences of using, implementing, or acting on what we just heard?" Even, "What would make this even more useful?" This conveys not only your investment but also your interest in the skill and insights available from your team.

What if nobody has the answer? This is often the case, but we rarely acknowledge it. Here you are, trying to create a new way of working together, and there is a lot that nobody knows much about yet. Rather than acting like you know, let your superpower be that you know how to figure it out together with your people. The design of such a meeting consists of three phases:

- ☐ Divergence.
- ☐ Emergence.
- ☐ Convergence.

Divergence

This is the phase when you open up a topic. The best way to do that is through questions that take you ever deeper below the surface. This is where the practice of asking powerful questions will be very useful to you. For example, let's assume that the burning issue is a recurring mistake that creates stress for your people as well as lost time and money for the company. The first question is of course how to fix this, how to stop repeating this error. However, if we stop here, we will only get the ideas that people already have prepared in their heads in advance of the meeting. The obvious answers might be: we'll create a checklist, pay more attention, write it in the job description, get new task management software, make a template to-do list, control more, inspect more, get more training. Sometimes one of these answers will be the solution. Most often when we have a recurring problem that puzzles us, we actually need to go deeper.

So how do you go deeper? You might ask unexpected questions, such as, "How will this mistake benefit us?" Or, "What is the hidden benefit that we don't acknowledge that leads us to recreate the situation again and again?" Even, "What is this recurring situation telling us about our true needs and desires?" Then, "How is that benefit important, and what other, less-damaging ways do we have to bring in this obviously needed benefit?" Can you feel it? These questions will open new possibilities, and lead eventually to new ways of solving the problem that neither you nor your people have thought of before. This kind of opening up the topic is what we call divergence.

Emergence

This is a time and space of uncertainty and creativity. Being in this emergent phase can feel out of the comfort zone at work, because people are used to a linear thinking process, especially in a corporate environment. People are accustomed to being presented to in a linear fashion, and to having linear thinking expected of them. Being in this emergent zone means getting comfortable with the questions, getting relaxed and playful with them, getting curious, and maybe even having a sense of humor about the unexpected responses. This stands in stark opposition to the common reactions to emergence. We have all been in meetings where stakeholders get frustrated about the seeming lack of efficiency when ready-made answers and solutions don't pop up fast enough.

Interestingly, it works in the exact opposite way. With a more relaxed approach, you and the entire group can get around the uncertainty of not knowing the answer (yet), and that means the more creative the answers and solutions will eventually be. So your job here, just like I mentioned earlier in chapter 3, is to hold the space. Both in the divergence and emergence phases, people need to experience trust and safety. In today's corporate culture, it is not normally safe not to know, not to have the answer, or even to risk asking a question that shows that we are not all-knowledgeable (or in agreement). Creating trust and safety in the core group and Sandbox group – and proving your sincerity – is therefore essential for the success of this process.

Convergence

This phase is the most familiar. You will be working out plans, next steps, concrete proposals, to-dos. Because of the collective, creative process that you had integrated before, the quality of the output in this phase will be much higher than it would had you jumped in straightaway after defining your first problem statement.

This three-phase structure is scalable. We will have many smaller such conversations that are part of a bigger project. You can look at the invitation to the Sandbox group, for example. Creating it is a conversation on its own. You will have a divergent, an emergent, and a convergent phase. The end result will be an invitation that will reflect the questions, creativity, and the spirit of the group creating it. It will be without a doubt much more inviting than the usual meeting invitations we get, and it will have a much greater impact as a result.

The tools that I share with you are created with this kind of architecture in mind.

Appreciative Inquiry

Appreciative Inquiry is a tool that I use often when there is a need to build trust, and bring to the surface the strengths and successes achieved as the basis for further development. Its core purpose is to help you consistently approach problem-solving from a constructive and positive perspective. It builds on the idea that when we study something (inquiry), when we pay lots of attention to it, it becomes stronger *just because* we are focusing our attention on it. In doing Appreciative Inquiry, we choose to look at the strengths and enabling factors, and by studying and learning about them, we create more of these positive attributes in the company or team. From this abundant base, Appreciative Inquiry gives us the tools to envision and plan the future that we want to achieve.

Appreciative Inquiry was developed at Case Western Reserve University by David Cooperrider and Suresh Srivastva. It is a very successful approach that has been used to create breakthroughs and improve the ways in which people relate to their work and their organizations around the world.

Appreciative inquiry is a methodology that can be used in small teams as well as with thousands of people.

You can think of Appreciative Inquiry as a tool or an approach. There is a lot you can achieve by adopting this approach, and the principles it is built on, in almost any project.

As a method, it can be summarized in the following steps:

Define phase:

Articulate your intention. What would you like to achieve?

Discovery phase:

Where do you have the attributes that will help you achieve it?

Here, your people will focus on discovering the best of what has happened in the past, as well as what is working well now (related, of course, to the intention or topic you yourself set for this session). The best way to do this is to start with the smaller group. Share success stories, and ask how people contributed to make those situations a success. Based on these few stories, sharpen your focus. What exactly are you looking for, looking to strengthen?

Next, you will formulate questions for a short interview guide, such as:

Tell me a story about a time when you felt that your work was very successful and you felt recognized and appreciated for it (it can be also from previous jobs).

What did you feel proudest about?

What from your gifts, talents, and attitudes contributed to that success?

What in the way the work is or was organized contributed to this success?

What values were demonstrated in this story?

The people in the group will split into pairs that will interview each other and take note of each other's answers. Then, they will come together in small groups of four to eight to share what they have learned. It is almost like you analyze the data that you gather to find out which company strengths relate to your inquiry, and what "ingredients" have made them possible.

Dream phase:

In this step, your group will look into the future. They will dream or envision what could be possible for your company. What results would be achieved if the strengths and talents that you just identified could express themselves more often, and if the success conditions would be always present? This is a moment to explore the possibilities. Think big, and get excited!

Design phase:

This phase takes the dream a step closer to reality. Together with your group, you're looking to define what it takes to make this dream possible. How would you need to support the company? How could you, as a group, make it work? It is a very practical, rational, and almost detailed part of the process, almost like project planning. You, as the group, will know at the end of it what to do, what resources you need, and what the next steps are to create your new reality.

Delivery phase:

This step is sometimes called "Destiny," and it is a very important phase. Sometimes the plans that you create in the Design phase are all you need, but more often, they represent just the beginning. Delivering the actual result may take further planning, coordination, and resources. This is the phase that brings about the actual change and the result you envisioned. Since this last step is not taking place in the safe environment of the Sandbox group, but in the "old world" of the broader culture, it will require a unique kind of nurturing and attention from your side, probably like some of the earlier initiatives born in the Sandbox group.

Appreciative Inquiry can help you discover treasures, build trust, and achieve results you never thought were possible – but only if people really go all in. Appreciative Inquiry opens amazing opportunities, and it is not difficult to implement. There is literature in every language dedicated to it, so if you want to dive in, you can. You can also work with an expert (especially if you plan to involve many people). With my clients, we start small, so they gradually learn how it works and where it is most valuable. Appreciative Inquiry becomes a tool that is always at their fingertips, to blast through blockades and build trust.

Open Space Technology

Have you ever been to a conference where you dozed off in the main-track sessions, only to have the most amazing conversations ever during the coffee break? The kind of conference where you can't remember much of the program, but you come away with great contacts, great (if accidental) insights, and even some great plans – with the people you met in the break. It's a success, even if you spent most of the time in the sessions checking your phone and catching up on work you brought from the office. If you recognize this scenario, it's because it's very common.

Harrison Owen had the genius idea, in the 1980s, of creating a way of meeting and talking to each other that brings all the benefits of the self-organization that you leverage in the coffee break into the conference room, so we never have to feel that we are only there for the breaks. This amazing, powerful methodology is called Open Space Technology.

What is it? It is a method for groups to self-organize, with lots of freedom to contribute to what they most care about, and initiate the ideas that they most want to explore and develop. It is also a marketplace where people get to learn, explore, give, and take. It is one of the most effective ways to focus and draw out creativity, inspire a sense of responsibility and ownership, and actualize results. It will go over well in a space such as the Sandbox group, and eventually even the entire company, but not right away, especially if the company has been obsessed by control and micromanagement.

I have seen it work all around the world in companies very diverse, big and small, as well as in NGOs and public administration.

There are four rules and one law, called the Law of the Two Feet. The four rules state:

1. Whoever comes are the right people.
2. Whatever happens is the only thing that could happen.
3. Whenever it starts it is the right time.
4. When it's over, it's over.

The Law of the Two Feet states: "If during the course of the gathering, any person finds themselves in a situation when they are neither learning nor contributing, they must use their feet and go to some more productive place." Here's how this process looks in a nutshell.

Step 1: Decide in advance the purpose of the open space. You can simply formulate it as a powerful question. This purpose statement (question) will also be the title of the open space.

Step 2: Invite your people. Open Space Technology can run with as few as 15 people, and as many as 2,000. However, if you have a group larger than 50 people, it does take special preparation. Invite those people who are likely to be the stakeholders in the issue or question that you are discussing.

Step 3. Set up the room. Prepare chairs in circles, and if there are too many people, arrange them in concentric circles. Prepare pens, markers, and paper to distribute. Also prepare an empty time table on the wall, with spaces and time slots in which to meet, such as depicted below. The empty squares in the timetable should be big enough so that people can stick papers in each. A4 or A5 (letter size) is most convenient in terms of size.

	Small Meeting Room 1	Big Room (table by window)	Big Room (sofas by the door)	Small Meeting Room 2	Lobby
9:30 - 10:15					
10:15 - 11:00					
11:00 - 11:45					

Step 4. Welcome the participants, and introduce them to the principles and the laws of the Open Space.

Step 5. Ask people to propose the topics they want to talk about. They don't need to be experts on it, they just need to be interested in exploring it. Write the topics and names on one paper, then stick them on the timetable.

Step 6. Take a deep breath and write. When you do it for the first time, this might be a scary moment, when you are wondering if anybody will propose anything. They always do. After a minute of hesitation, someone will break the ice, and proposals will flow in.

What to do if there are more proposals then timeslots? Sometimes, you can group two topics together if they fit, but I wouldn't try too hard for that kind of efficiency. If it is not an easy, natural fit (only the people who propose the topics can decide), then leave it. Choose the topics on a first-come, first-served basis.

Step 7. Now you have an exact timetable, and everybody is free to choose the conversation(s) in which they participate. The hosts – the people who propose the topic – need to make sure that some notes and conclusions are written down. Also remind these hosts that their role is to ask questions and engage people, not to lecture them and dominate the conversation. Remind the other people to stay only for as long as they find it useful.

Step 8. After that, the event mostly runs itself. When I facilitate an Open Space, I do circulate among people and remind them of the timing when a session is up, but not much more.

The job here is to "hold the space." Trust that it works, believe in the people, and be present for any questions that might arise.

Step 9. Leave 40 minutes at the end to come back together in order to share the impressions and learning from the open space. You will be surprised by the richness of the conversation, the amazing ideas, and creativity that is made manifest.

Open Space Technology is quite easy to run, and it's a brilliant way to bring together shareholders and technical leaders for projects, find creative solutions, and more – all by learning and building strong relationships among people.

You can go much more in-depth in learning about this method. While it is not a difficult process, its success does depend on preparation as well as some intangibles, such as the degree of trust that you hold. Remember what I said in chapter 3: the quality of the space depends on the inner state of the person holding it. In all the methods I am presenting here, this is true –and probably nowhere more than in the use of Open Space Technology.

If you want to explore more about this method, a great resource is Harrison Owen's book, *Open Space Technology*. If you have questions about this or any of the methods, drop me a line and we can talk about how you can use that.

World Café

World Café is an easy-to-use method for creating very dynamic, engaging, and creative conversations that also connect and inspire each other. It is a great way to bring out the intelligence and the creativity of the room on a given topic. It has the advantage of getting incredible results very fast. I have witnessed people who have never met before quickly and completely immersed in great conversations.

It brings to the workplace the feel of a café conversation with our best friends, or late-night bar conversations with college buddies, about changing the world. Remember those?

What if there were a way to have an amazing, deep, meaningful, and productive conversation with anybody – *right away?* World Café delivers on that.

World Café adheres to seven design principles:

Set the context. The first question that you need to answer is: Why are you bringing people together? What is the purpose? Once you have that, it will be easy to know who the people should be. What will be the best question to ask? Also consider how many rounds of conversation you want to have, and for how long.

Create hospitable space. This refers to physical and psychological space. Create an invitation that sets the tone. Make sure that the room feels comfortable, and that people feel safe and relaxed.

Explore questions that matter. Use powerful questions to elicit people's insights and creativity. You can use only one question, or if you have enough time, questions that build on each other.

Encourage everyone's contribution. The Café, in small groups, makes it easier for people to talk, but it's still important to emphasize conversation. They are also free to participate only by listening, if this is what they choose.

Connect diverse perspectives. Here, like in Open Space Technology, people will get the opportunity to participate in more than one conversation. This is a great asset as they get to candid questions, insight, and perspectives from one conversation to another. This kind of sharing accelerates discoveries and increases awareness of possibilities.

Listen together for patterns and insights. Listening with great attention to each other is what really makes a difference in these conversations. Conversation is not only about speaking, but, even more importantly, about listening. When we listen together, we find that we are treasures, so encourage everybody to offer one another the valuable gift of listening.

Share collective discoveries. The World Café conversation encourages insights and *aha* moments. Share them with the group, because they are part of the collective intelligence that emerges in this context.

This is how you organize a World Café at a glance.

Seat four (a maximum of five) people at small tables.

Set up three progressive rounds of conversations, each about 20 minutes' duration. For each round, craft a powerful question on topics that generally matter to most people.

Encourage participants to take notes, doodle, or draw collectively on the paper prepared on their table.

After the first round of conversation, ask people to disperse and move to other tables. You may ask one of them to stay and act as a host to the next group, somebody who will act as a guardian of the developing conversation.

After the three rounds of conversation, take time to come together again in a circle to share discoveries, insights, and experiences. This is a further opportunity to see emerging patterns and possibilities for action.

The best resource to learn more about World Café is Juanita's Brown book, *The World Café: Shaping Our Future Through Conversations That Matter.*

Pro Action Café

Pro Action Café is a combination of Open Space Technology and World Café. Like in the Open Space, participants get to propose topics that matter to them. Like in World Café, you have three rounds of progressive conversation – only this time, each table has a different topic. The host will be the person who proposed the topic.

I use Pro Action Café to explore and gather insights, ideas, and perspectives on a variety of topics, and to generate new possibilities for action – all very quickly. It is an amazing method, because just like World Café, it creates valuable conversation very fast, and brings out the best in people. Also, I find that by engaging in this kind of conversation, people see each other in a new light – and relationships are strengthened. Pro Action Café was developed in Brussels by Ria Baeck and Rainer von Leoprechting. I witnessed that development process firsthand, and I am very happy to be part of the incredible journey of Pro Action Café around the globe.

The flow of Pro Action Café:

Set aside 2.5 to 3 hours for the Café.

Start by having a short, welcoming check-in circle (you can read more about check-in later in this chapter). Count the number of participants, and then divide by four. That will give you the number of projects or questions that you can work on, or the number of conversations you can have in this session.

Invite people, just like in Open Space, to propose a topic or a project for conversation. The only criteria is that this topic is meaningful and important to them. If the Café has a specific purpose, then of course the project will have to be somehow related to the larger purpose. If more projects and ideas are proposed than you have tables, take them for consideration on a first-come, first-serve basis.

When the topics are identified, ask each host who proposed a topic to go and sit at one of the tables. The other people will join those conversations according to what interests them most.

There will be three rounds, so all the travelers can participate in at least three different topics. Each round takes about 20 minutes, maximum 30, and it has a focus question.

Round 1: What is the question behind the core question? This is a question for divergence, for opening up and deepening the inquiry for more understanding of the need and the purpose of the conversation.

Round 2: What is missing? In this round, we are looking for new perspectives and ways of making the project more complete.

Round 3: What am I learning about myself? What am I learning about my project? What next steps will I take? These are questions for convergence, helping to forge specific action from the results of the conversation.

After each round, the travelers will stand up and move to another topic of their interest. Take a short break between rounds, so that people can move about in a relaxed way, pick up a coffee or tea on the way back, and come together in a new group to talk about the next topic in the new round.

Finally, gather together again in a big circle, like in the beginning, and share key insights, learning, and aha moments – both from the travelers and the hosts.

Check-In and Check-Out

Check-ins and check-outs are fast methods that present a great way to bring the group together and set an intimate atmosphere of trust and sharing. The process is easy and it doesn't have to take a long time. Here is how you do it:

Gather all the people in the room into a circle, if possible.

Welcome everyone and share the purpose, the calling question for the meeting. Introduce the check-in by telling everyone how much time is allocated for that, so that people know if they only have time for a word, a sentence, or more.

Introduce the check-in/-out question, which should be one that all participants can answer, such as: "What am I excited about in being here?" "Why is it important for me to be here today?" "What treasure did I find today, here, that I am taking back with me?" Sometimes you can also use a metaphor, such as: "If you were a color, what color would you be, and why?"

Facilitate listening, and ensure that people don't interrupt each other. You can do that beautifully by using a talking piece. A talking piece can be any object: a pen, a stone, maybe something small that has special meaning to your group. Anybody who has the talking piece can speak, and all others will listen. When the speaker is finished, they will put the talking piece down, or hand it to the next person. It is a small instrument, and a very simple one with a great power. It creates an atmosphere of concentration and respectful listening.

These very simple methods set the tone at the beginning of a meeting, and also help close the meeting in a beautiful way. They are really important also to mark that you are opening a new kind of conversation in a new kind of space.

The Advice Process

The Advice Process is a gem that stuns through simplicity, elegance, and effectiveness. It is not a method for conducting a conversation, but rather a method of taking initiative and making decisions within the company. It is your new way of thinking about people and work, in action.

The Advice Process is an instrument that gives people in the company a great deal of trust, initiative, and power. It also ensures that all action will be taken with enough information and advice.

For most companies this sounds absurd, the stuff of fairy tales: "You mean everybody can have an idea and implement it? Just like this? Sounds like a recipe for chaos and disaster!" The answer is: Yes, they can do it! And no, it's not at all chaotic, it is actually very systematic. Here is how they do it:

Somebody has an idea on how to improve something, large or small (a work process, a product, marketing).

Now, they need to gather intelligence on the various aspects of implementing the idea.

They will ask for advice from those within the company, and possibly outside, who will in some way be impacted by the change that they are proposing, or from those that have experience in that sort of thing. If these are too many people, they have to make sure to at least ask advice from one member of every category of stakeholders.

The Advice Process

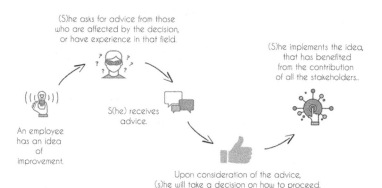

(S)he asks for advice from those who are affected by the decision, or have experience in that field.

(S)he implements the idea, that has benefited from the contribution of all the stakeholders..

An employee has an idea of improvement.

S(he) receives advice.

Upon consideration of the advice, (s)he will take a decision on how to proceed. (S)he does not have to follow the advice.

Below is a chart about how much advice you would need in relation to the importance of the decision.

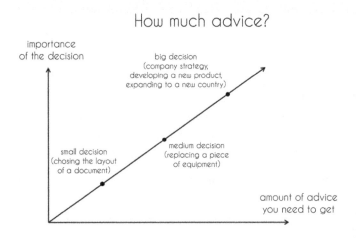

How much advice?

importance of the decision

big decision
(company strategy,
developing a new product,
expanding to a new country)

small decision
(chosing the layout
of a document)

medium decision
(replacing a piece
of equipment)

amount of advice
you need to get

After gathering all the insight and advice, they (the employee who had the idea) make a decision about going ahead (or not). The decision will be informed by the advice they get, but they don't have to follow the advice. They make the decision according to their best judgment.

They go ahead and implement their idea (with the support of the company), improving their idea based on the feedback and contributions they get along the way.

There are many accounts of business successes that came from the "shop floor." The advice process puts creativity and drive for improvement in the center of the business, rather than leaving it to chance, or driving it from the top or the side.

By giving the people the actual power to decide and to implement change within the company, you ensure engagement and initiative. And what if it doesn't work out? That can happen . . . but it will happen less often than in those companies where the decisions are taken by the management and imposed on those who carry out the change.

Collective Story Harvesting

This is a wonderful thing to do when you or several people within or even outside your company have experience that can be a source of learning for your people. I first encountered this method in the work of Mary Alice Arthur, who has also developed an in-depth guide for it (see the back of this book for references). I have used it dozens of times, always with great success, because it is such an easy and powerful way to learn, inspire, and grow. Because it taps into the ancient power of storytelling, people love it.

Here is how to do it in a nutshell.

Allow 90 minutes' time.

Chose a story carefully, so it is relevant to what the group wants to learn about. The best person to tell the story is always somebody who was part of the story.

Welcome the audience, and introduce the story as well as the purpose of the session. Prepare the audience by asking them to choose a certain angle to listen for, a certain "story thread." That will give everybody a chance to listen carefully for specific aspects. Possible threads to choose from (but you can always choose your own specific theme):

Narrative thread: The thread of the story – people, events, stages. You might also capture facts, emotions, and values that are part of the story.

Process: What interventions, processes, applications, or discoveries happened?

Pivotal points: When did breakthroughs occur? What did we learn?

Application: What can we learn from this story to apply to our own or other systems?

Taking change to scale: What can we learn from this story about taking change to scale?

Questions: What questions arise from this story that we could ask ourselves?

When things just came together: What where the times when the right people showed up and things just flowed naturally?

Principles: What principles of working can be gleaned from this story?

Challenges encountered: Describe, and include discussion of how they were overcome.

Storytelling: ask the storyteller to tell the story. At the same time, the audience will take notes based on their specific thread.

Ask the audience to share what they have been listening for, and what they have learned. Take as much time for this part as you took for the story itself.

Give the floor back to the storyteller, and ask them what they are learning from the audience. It is always very interesting to see how this "field of listening" creates new insights – even for the people who were part of the story, but have never reflected on it just like that.

Thank the storyteller and the audience, and close the session.

... and Many More

These are some of my favorite "tools" for increasing engagement, trust, and positive results within a workplace culture. There are of course many more, but the ones in this chapter are a good place to start to create a beautiful experience of creativity and learning in the Sandbox group (and any other group in your company).

Here, as well, I encourage you to look for support: maybe some people in your company already have experience with some of these methods. If so – use it! You can also reach out for expert support, especially when you use these methods for the first time. But in the short term, I encourage you to make it a priority to build this capability in your company. These methods are magical: you'll be astounded by the quality of the conversation, the results, and the great atmosphere that develops in the group when you use them.

NEXT

While we have arrived at the end of the book, you are not at the end of this work. The steps and tools that I described in chapters 3 through 6 are practices. That means these are things you need to practice regularly, just like you practice any new activity or habit, like going to the gym.

You don't get to just challenge your limiting beliefs once and be done with it, for example. Becoming aware and intentional about our thoughts, instead of allowing ourselves to remain on autopilot, is a lifelong practice. The same applies to all the other steps. If you put this intention at the core of your work, the rest will easily flow from there.

As you learn more and more about the real nature of your people, as you learn to trust them with their areas of responsibility, a lot of the "busy-ness" that stems from the need to micromanage and control others' daily assignments falls aside. You will have more time for the parts of the business that fill you with excitement.

After a time, these practices will become second nature, the natural way you do things. At this point, you are no longer *doing* this work, you *have become* this work, and you are in an easy flow with the work.

As you well know, your company is in constant change. To stay still means to become obsolete, and very fast. You now have a way to be in constant movement, and to adapt, innovate, attract, and retain the best talent – with ease and joy.

My wish for you is to get started – and to be inspired to continue!

Reading this book is good. Applying what you have learned is so much better. It will make all the difference. I have prepared a roadmap to guide you, and you can download this for free at www.theceosplaybook.com

Here is some heartfelt advice: Don't struggle alone. Getting your head around this work can be daunting at first. Many of the CEOs who pioneered this work, as well as many of my clients who have successfully walked this path, consider having a guide or mentor by their side to be one of their most important success factors.

I wish you and your people a lot of joy on this exciting and exhilarating ride to discover all the ways in which your company can thrive while making the world a better place.

References

Art of Hosting Conversations that Matter: http://www.artofhosting.org

Brian M. Carney and Isaac Getz, Freedom, Inc.: *How Corporate Liberation Unleashes Employee Potential and Business Performance*

Byron Katie, *Loving What Is: Four Questions That Can Change Your Life*

Daniel Pink, *Drive: The Surprising Truth About What Motivates Us*

Diana D. Whitney (Author), Amanda Trosten – Bloom, *The Power of Appreciative Inquiry: A Practical Guide to Positive Change*

Eric Vogt, Juanita Brown and David Isaacs, *The Art of Powerful Questions* (get it here: http://www.theworldcafe.com/tools-store/store/)

Frederic Laloux, *Reinventing Organizations: A Guide to Creating Organizations Inspired by the Next Stage of Human Consciousness*

Gallup State of the American Workplace Report (http://www.gallup.com/services/178514/state-american-workplace.aspx)

Harrison H. Owen, *Open Space Technology: A User's Guide*

Juanita Brown, *The World Café: Shaping Our Futures Through Conversations That Matter*

Mary Alice Arthur, David Hanna: "Collective Story Harvest" (http://goo.gl/LvKWvU)

Peter Block, *The Answer to How Is Yes: Acting on What Matters*

Pro Action Café: http://uccommunity.org.au/sites/default/files/the_proaction_cafe.pdf

About the Author

Author photo courtesy
of Timothi Jane Graham

Dr. Nora Ganescu is a coach, consultant, and trainer.

Her work is helping companies maximize their impact and become amazing workplaces, where people love to contribute at their fullest.

Nora started her professional journey 25 years ago as a youth activist for intercultural understanding in post-communist Romania, and she has been dedicated to building bridges between people ever since. She went on to work with thousands of employees and executives in companies, NGOs, in public administration, and international organizations, as an external and internal consultant in over 30 countries and across three continents. Lufthansa, Habitat for Humanity, European Commission, and the National Academy for Public Administration are but a few examples.

Nora is a passionate learner, always exploring the frontier of her discipline to bring her clients the best combination of time-tested wisdom and cutting-edge thinking. In her work, she combines personal development tools, spiritual nourishment from ancient wisdom, schools, and insights gleaned from some of the most forward-looking and successful companies in the world.

Nora's clients are CEOs who are ready to stop struggling with their people and want an easier, healthier, and more effective path to success.

Nora loves to spend time with her family, read, travel, and (lately) run half-marathons.

Get Your Free Road Map

Thank you for reading this book. I have prepared an online and downloadable set of tools to get you started. The tools include:

• A calculator that gives you an accurate estimate of how much money you could save if you engage your people – and how much you waste every year if you don't. (Tip: you can use this to strengthen your business case for change).

• A short quiz that will give you a picture of where your management model excels and struggles as of right now.

• A visual roadmap, so that you know what to do at each step at a glance.

• Meeting templates for your Sandbox group meetings.

• A 30-minute strategy session with me, so that you are set up for a successful start.

You can download them all for free. It's easy so do this right now:

1. Simply go to www.theceosplaybook.com
2. Put in your first name and primary email address
3. Click the button provided

Don't wait. Start building your Dream Team today.

Morgan James
Speakers Group

www.TheMorganJamesSpeakersGroup.com

We connect Morgan James published
authors with live and online events
and audiences whom will benefit
from their expertise.

Morgan James makes all of our titles available
through the Library for All Charity Organization.

www.LibraryForAll.org

9 781683 503101